His *Faithfulness* is in the Waiting

Finding Intimacy with Father God through the Psalms

MARJ HOTELLING

Dedication

I dedicate this book to my husband: an example of honor, integrity, and a man willing to be transformed into God's image. In fact, I don't know of any other person who has changed so much as you. I have the utmost respect for you. Thank you for encouraging me to write this book, but most of all, thank you for giving me permission to allow both of our lives to be transparent so others may experience God's faithfulness in the waiting.

Contents

Foreword

But, as it is written, "What no eye has seen, nor ear heard, nor the heart of man imagined, what God has prepared for those who love him"—these things God has revealed to us through the Spirit. For the Spirit searches everything, even the depths of God (1 Corinthians 2:9-10 ESV).

These two verses are a tremendous promise, an incredible thought that God has so much to give to anyone who allows the Spirit of God to reveal such things to them. In life's journey we come across individuals who have been in the Spirit, and in the Spirit things have been revealed; so it is with Marj Hotelling! After reading her book and knowing Marj as her pastor, I believe that the Spirit of God has given her insight. She has been able to reveal valuable insight from life experiences and form them into lessons about the relationship between God and His creation.

His Faithfulness Is in the Waiting is an inspiring journey! Whoever reads this book will find themselves walking in the footsteps of freedom, healing, and love. I believe Marj's eyes have seen and her ears have heard, and God has revealed to her heart the things prepared for her—and not only for her, but also for you!

I know that Marj's book will bring you to a greater understanding of the Father's unfailing love!

—Rev. David Forsythe
Founding and Senior Pastor, Third Day Worship Centre
Syracuse, New York

Introduction

I have loved hanging out with David in the Psalms. Through the ages he has been known as "a man after God's own heart," and I want to be known as a woman after God's own heart. You become who you hang around with and I've hung out with David in the Psalms day after day for many years. David's proclamation and the theme that is woven through the Psalms is the message of God's faithfulness. I have been overwhelmed and even perplexed at times with God's faithfulness in my own life. You see, God's love is an everyday occurrence; it's in the little things,—in the everyday monotonous, routine, weariness of life when we experience God's faithfulness. It's in our discouragement, anxieties, and fears—always constant, never changing. That's how our circumstances change, and, most importantly, that's how we change; by experiencing the love and faithfulness of God in the everyday things.

I had to trust God that He was going to change my husband and that He would be faithful to love him and deliver him, and to heal his wounded soul. As I look back, what impacted my husband the most was the day-to-day display of my Father's faithfulness.

As my husband was changing he had to wait for me to change to be able to trust him again. He studied and prayed through Ephesians, "Husbands love your wives as Christ loves the church." What was my Abba doing in me? He was developing my faith, healing my wounded soul, developing my character, teaching me how to love and how to forgive—both myself and others—and I was developing an intimate relationship with Him and a love for His Word, His Love Book. During the waiting, He used my journey through the Psalms to help me change and to get to know Him intimately as my Daddy.

God's faithfulness brought about restored lives that bring glory to Him because, you see, that's what our Daddy does—He restores everything that has been lost and everything that has been broken. And you, too, can experience that His faithfulness is in the waiting.

Chapter 1: Why is it so Cold in Here?

The baby girl loved being in her Grandpa's arms, and this day was no different. She clung to him with squeals of delight as he carried her into her parent's living room. However, the surroundings were not familiar and she snuggled into her grandfather's neck because of the chill in the room. And then the eleven-month-old girl spotted someone lying down with a bandage wrapped around their head and she began to hang on a little tighter to her grandfather's suit coat. Ah! But then as Grandpa drew closer, the baby recognized this man; it was her dear daddy! Filled with glee, she threw out her arms to him and tried to wriggle out of the older man's embrace, but she didn't know that her dear father's kisses and hugs were never to be experienced again. His body was lying lifeless in a casket. Her grandfather held her tightly, and as people were overcome with grief they began sobbing uncontrollably as the baby was whisked out of the room.

The year was 1953, and it was the custom to have deceased bodies displayed in the home. And so it was with this dear father of six young children who was tragically killed in an automobile accident from severe head injuries. All the furniture had to be moved out of the living room to make space for the casket. There was no heat coming out of the coal furnace on that frigid December day in order for the body to be kept cold.

I was that eleven-month-old baby girl. My life changed forever as death took my father at the age of thirty-two. I was to grow up without a father, searching and yearning for that unconditional love of security, acceptance, and approval—and many times finding it in all the wrong places.

I had given my life to Jesus when I was ten years old, but chose to live my life as I pleased. I knew my sins were forgiven and that God loved me, but I left Him, thinking I knew what was best for my life.

At the age of twenty-nine I received news that my husband had died of a massive coronary, and I became a widow with two young sons. I laid on the floor, drenching the carpet with my tears until there were no more tears within me. It was then that I cried out to God whom I had so blatantly rebelled against for the last nineteen years! And He was there! He assured me of His forgiveness and His love once again, that there was nothing so horrible that I had done which He would not forgive. His faithfulness was in the waiting.

I learned of His mercy and great grace as He gave me another husband and four more children. And that span of time is what I have recorded in this account of my search for a Daddy and the intimacy and divine romance I have found with Father God through the Psalms, and this is what I have built my life upon: *His faithfulness is in the waiting.*

Chapter 2: Daddy's Love Letter

To My Daddy, the Father Who Will Never Leave Me or Forsake Me

I never got to write a letter to my father or send him a Father's Day card, so I wrote a letter to Father God, my Abba Daddy, and I put it in my Bible. I take it out every now and then, especially when fear attacks and discouragement and anxiety begin to overwhelm me. It gives me faith, courage, strength, and hope that He will be faithful to me once again while I am waiting.

Dearest Daddy,

I'm so happy that I can call You that! I was reading in Your Love Letter to me that You actually want me to call You that. And of all Your many, many names, this is still my favorite: Daddy.

Thank You for loving me through every change in my life and for putting me in the most secure secret hiding place of all while I was changing—You have put me "in Christ" so that Your unchanging, unconditional, perfect, unfailing love could surround me as I grew up in You.

Out of all the great and precious promises that You have taught me, the one I have clung to the most is Your promise that You will never leave me or forsake me. You know that I searched in many places for someone who would never hurt, disappoint, or betray me, but all I found was disappointment and sorrow. Sometimes it so damaged and injured me that it wounded and penetrated my very soul. Oh, how desperate I was! It was a long process, Daddy, but You were waiting with Your arms outstretched. Your faithfulness was surely in the waiting.

You opened my blind eyes so I could see the cross where Your Son died to forgive my sins, taking my shame and guilt. Please forgive me for taking so long—this is the only regret that I have in this journey with You—that I wasted so much time! But there You were, waiting just for me and loving me unconditionally—totally, fully, and absolutely. I experienced the fullness of Your unqualified, unreserved, unrestricted, unquestioning love, and that love reached back into my past—into all my brokenness—and restored and healed me, taking all of my ashes and making them into something beautiful. You have even promised in Your Love Letter that You will restore the time that I lost when I was searching. Thank You for being so patient and longsuffering with me. Somehow, "thank you" just doesn't seem to be enough for this love relationship with You, My Daddy! Your faithfulness was in the waiting.

Sometimes I was confused about the discipline that You brought into my life, but then I learned I had to go through the refiner's fire until Your reflection—Your image—was seen in my life. I thought You had forgotten me and didn't hear my cries. I thought that I was surely going to die, but then I remembered that great promise that You would never leave me. You were teaching me how to love and forgive my enemies—but the hardest of all was learning how to forgive myself. I learned to trust You, and I discovered in Your Word that You will sit as a refiner and purifier of silver. I knew it! You were sitting there with me the whole time; You promised to never leave me, and You are always doing what is best for me, because that's what Daddies do! Your faithfulness was in the waiting.

You taught me who You are in your Love Letter through the Psalms of your beloved David. Then I learned that You call me Your beloved Pearl. I want to recount back to you some of things you taught me through David's love letters to You. I know, Daddy, that You never get tired of me telling You how much I love You, and I will never tire of hearing how much You love me.

Not only have I learned who you are through the Psalms, but You have told me who I am in You. I am like a tree planted by streams of water which yields its fruit in season and whose leaf does not wither, whatever I do prospers, for You watch over me! There it is again; You will never leave me. You say to me, "There's no need to be afraid, Daughter, I will never leave you."

You have rescued me and saved me because You delight in me. You say I am free, approved of, accepted, loved, worthy, beautiful, safe, secure, and anointed. In fact, You have made me brand new and call me Your daughter—I belong to You!

You have taught me to speak hope to my soul, just like David did, when discouragement and depression begin to try to make their home in my heart and rob me of the promises I have believed in Your Love Book.

Even as I write this love letter to honor You, thoughts flood my mind so rapidly I cannot write this out fast enough or recount all the things You have taught me, or all the ways You love me. You have taught me how to worship You and how Your presence refreshes my soul. This has become the passion of my life, and I have joyfully discovered that Your presence is my greatest need! Oh, if only I could express myself in worship even more than I already do! But how can I ever express my love and gratitude to You, Daddy, for everything You are to me?

You have given me a new heart. I remember when I was reading your Love Letter that Your beloved David said that You are close to the brokenhearted. How I wept when I read that astounding promise and oh how I clung to it and believed with all my heart that You were close to me. I believed You because I know You always do what You say You will do. And in Your great faithfulness, and in the waiting, You healed and restored me, and gave meaning and purpose to my life.

Your presence is my greatest need, whether it's drinking my cup of coffee with You in the morning or experiencing Your manifest presence in corporate worship. The highest calling is that I might live there, in Your presence, and gaze upon Your beauty all the days of my life.

Oh, and this one, Daddy, is one of my favorites: You renew my youth as the eagle's and You satisfy my desires with good things. Who can ever comprehend that I can have such intimacy with the God who created the universe, and that You would satisfy my every desire. This is all because You made a way through Your Son.

I lie down and sleep in peace, and then wake again because You have watched over me, just like a Dad—my protector, I never have to fear again. You make me strong and courageous, and You have taught me not to be afraid because You are always with me and will never leave me.

The light of Your face shines upon me and fills me with joy. You even have named me Your Pearl because that's what my name means. Pearls are the only gem that live and mature in a living environment. My life is in You—I live and breathe because of Your life in me.

Morning by morning You hear me as I call out my requests before You and wait in expectation for You to answer because Your faithfulness is in the waiting.

I take refuge in You and I am glad, I will ever sing for joy because You spread Your protection over me. Surely You bless the righteous, and that's me—Your Pearl! You surround me with Your favor like a shield everywhere I go.

Daddy, I don't even know how to end this love letter to You because there's so much more that I could say. I know that I am Your only child and the apple of Your eye, and if You gave me one request it would be that my life would bring glory to you! I'm looking forward in confident expectation to the abundant life every day because I know You are with me and You will never leave me, and that Your faithfulness is always in the waiting.

Nothing can ever separate me from your love again.

Your Loving Daughter,

Your Pearl

Chapter 3: Character Matters

Lord, who dares to dwell with you? Who presumes the privilege of being close to you, living next to you in your shining place of glory? Who are those who daily dwell in the life of the Holy Spirit? They are passionate and wholehearted, always sincere and always speaking the truth—for their hearts are trustworthy. They refuse to slander or insult others; they'll never listen to gossip or rumors, nor would they ever harm another with their words. They will speak out passionately against evil and evil workers while commending the faithful ones who follow after the truth. They make firm commitments and follow through, even at great cost. They never crush others with exploitation or abuse and they would never be bought with a bribe against the innocent. They will never be shaken; they will stand firm forever (Psalm 15 TPT).

Father God told me in my early walk with Him that His initial and foremost concern for me as His daughter was that I develop godly character.

In fact, this is what He said to me:

"I am more concerned about your attitude and your willful motives than I am about your abilities, because this is what forms your character. You see, Pearl, I gave you your abilities and your gifts; I already know what you're capable of. I also gave you a will, a choice, to love Me. I wait with expectation for you to lay your will on the altar. Change the "I will" and lay it down before the "I AM." I will stretch you beyond what you think you're capable of. All things are possible with Me. Humble yourself before Me, and I will lift you up. Lay down your life for the One who gave you His."

God is more concerned that my soul within me is set free than He is with the circumstances that surround me. But somehow He used my circumstances to change me. While I was waiting for my circumstances to change, He was faithful to change me. His faithfulness was in the waiting, developing my character. He reached back into my past with His great love, and took all the negative things in my life (some from my own bad decisions) and He took what was meant for evil and made it into something good! Only a loving, devoted Father could do that! My Daddy God gave me many practical lessons about attitude adjustments. I am a work in progress and sometimes I fail, but He picks me back up again and tells me, "Daughter, we're going to try this again!" It's like a kid learning to ride a bike—I never get to fail, I just get to do it again!

"Tear up that List"

Lord, who dares to dwell with you? Who presumes the privilege of being close to you, living next to you in your shining place of glory? Who are those who daily dwell in the life of the Holy Spirit? (Psalm 15:1 TPT).

One morning I was praying and reading a list I had written about things I wanted God to fix about my husband. The Lord spoke clearly to me and said, "Tear up that list! It is just a list of complaints about your husband." So I quickly learned that any list—written or in my mind, will not be a complaint list. Complaining is like an undertow in the water; it will quickly drown and suffocate me in a grave of discouragement. Complaining (whining or grumbling) only produces anxiety, irritability, depression, discouragement, and a broken relationship with my Lord! His Love Book says that the Israelites complained against God, and the result was that they had to wander in the desert for forty years. The desert is hot, dry, and miserable—there's no life in the desert! God has taught me that complaining will bring the same results in my life. So when I am worn out, irritable, tired, and weary in my misery because I was grumbling and complaining, I ask forgiveness and repent—turn away from my complaining—and instead give God all my anxiety and cares!

> Don't be pulled in different directions or worried about a thing. Be saturated in prayer throughout each day, offering your faith-filled requests before God with overflowing gratitude. Tell him every detail of your life, then God's wonderful peace that transcends human understanding will make the answers known to you through Jesus Christ (Philippians 4:6-7 TPT).

What a wonderful discovery from the Word of God! I can talk to the Lord whenever I want, just like sitting at the feet of a devoted father—He is such a good listener! And before He answers my requests, I am filled with thankfulness and peace calms my heart and mind because I know that *His faithfulness is in the waiting!*

> My fellow believers, when it seems as though you are facing nothing but difficulties see it as invaluable opportunity to experience the greatest joy that you can! For you know that when your faith is tested it stirs up power within you to endure all things (James 1:2-3 TPT).

This early training laid a foundation for me that I have built on every day. It lays a foundation of endurance and holiness because I am passionate and desire to grow in holiness just as David was. From when I get up in the morning until I lie my head on my pillow I am thankful because *His faithfulness is in the waiting!*

Slam That Door Shut

Beloved, when we murmur and complain we open a door to the enemy. Let's take a closer look at this. One way to define *complaining* is to express grief, pain or discontentment, dissatisfaction, or resentment. Remember that our words are so very important that scripture tells us they can bring life or they can bring death (Proverbs 18:21).

When we complain about any situation in our lives that we are dissatisfied with, it is a very big deal. We have just given the enemy the right to steal our joy, peace, love, and hope. Our words are like seeds—and we've just planted them in the soil of unforgiveness and bitterness. And every time we voice our complaint to others, we keep watering that soil. What we are really saying is, "I don't think God can fix this in my life." We are sowing words of doubt and unbelief.

Researchers have found that when people complain they actually feel worse afterward. Sometimes we like to gloss it over and say things like, "I'm just venting." Scientific studies have found that happy people complain less.

Would you believe that our Daddy actually *wants* us to bring our concerns, fears, longings to Him? Don't go to other people with those complaints; He desires you to have such an intimate relationship with Him that you can trust Him with anything. Only He has the power to solve problems, soften people's hearts, and surround us with compassion. He is waiting for us to pour out our hearts to Him, and as we wait expectantly, He will give us peace. This is the intimacy that is developed in the day-to-day ordinary things of life.

David modeled this for us in Psalm 142:1-3 (TPT):

> God, I'm crying out to you! I lift up my voice boldly to beg for your mercy. I spill out my heart to you and tell you all my troubles. For when I was desperate, overwhelmed and about to give up you were the only one there to help. You gave me a way of escape from the hidden traps of my enemies.

Don't Get Caught in the Trap!

Complaining is a trap of the enemy, remember he comes to steal, kill, and destroy. Let me give you an example of this.

I have been in meetings where the Holy Spirit was moving powerfully. In these meetings there are ministry teams of people who are gifted in words of knowledge, wisdom, and prophecy. It is extremely exciting to witness people's lives being changed because of the great love of our Father. What are we to do with these powerful words that have come from the throne room?

First of all, write them down immediately or record them on a recording device, because the enemy will try to steal them immediately. Paul told young Timothy to battle well with the prophecies that were spoken over him (I Tim. 1:18). This means that whenever you have doubt in your mind, you are to talk back to the enemy of your soul using the words that were spoken over you. Sadly, I have seen people who received amazing words that could change their lives, only to leave the meeting and immediately begin complaining about their situation, health, husband, children, mother, or whatever they were dissatisfied with. The enemy just stole the word from them that could have brought greatness, relief, and solutions to their problems.

Beloved, God loves faith, not doubt. When we trust Him, He takes great pleasure in us. He brings the greatness out in us! Refuse to complain and criticize. My mind still has not been able to process what God sees in me, but I am pursuing this with a passion.

If you have found yourself complaining or criticizing, do not come under condemnation, but under the conviction of the Holy Spirit. Follow these seven steps to come back into peace:

1. Read Lamentations 3:19-25. Remember that complaining will not comfort or produce a destiny of blessing.

2. Repent. Ask the Lord to change you! Tell God how sorry you are for putting another person on the altar to put your hope in and meet your needs. He loves us so much that He won't allow anyone else to step into His place. Ask forgiveness for putting this burden on another person.

3. Put the Word in your mouth. Find promises that pertain to your problem and begin speaking them over yourself.

4. Seek approval from God—not others—and pull down this stronghold.

5. Ask the Holy Spirit daily to put a guard over your mouth (Ps. 141:3). This will keep the door shut to the enemy.

6. Forgive, pray, and bless the person you were complaining about.

7. Wait expectantly for God to change your situation.

A God-Approved List

> They are passionate and wholehearted, always sincere and always speaking the truth—for their hearts are trustworthy (Psalm 15:2 TPT).

God calls the things that are not as though they were (Rom. 4:17 KJV). He taught me how to speak His promises and believe them. Inheriting God's promises depends entirely on faith. You have to believe in faith, confidently trusting in God that His Word is powerful and it will accomplish what it sets out to do. Look what Isaiah 55:11 (KJV) says:

> So shall my word be that goeth forth out of my mouth: it shall not return unto me void, but it shall accomplish that which I please, and it shall prosper in the thing whereto I sent it.

God called Abraham a father of many nations before he even had a son, and before Abraham even believed Him. He gave life to that which was dead. Because we are made in His image, when we speak His Word, it will also give life to that which does not exist yet. How long are we to speak it and believe? Until it becomes obvious that it has accomplished what it was set out to do.

The Lord helped me tailor make a list that He approved of for my husband from His Word of Love, and He told me to believe in faith that He would save my marriage. I wrote down God's words in my journal and on index cards to carry around with me so they would be accessible wherever I had a moment to read them: stopped in traffic, cooking a meal, early in the morning, and late at night. I decreed His promises over my husband and believed that they would accomplish that very thing. My faith began to increase as I spoke the Word out loud. Here are some of the things that God instructed me to call my husband:

- Free (John 8:36)
- Healed (Jer. 30:17)
- Anointed (I John 2:20)
- A great man of God, fulfilling his destiny (Jer. 29:11)
- My husband is respected at the city gates (Proverbs 31:23)
- He is standing firm like a flourishing tree planted by God's design, deeply rooted by the brooks of bliss, bearing fruit in every season of his life. He is never dry, never fainting, ever blessed, ever prosperous. (Psalm 1:3 TPT)
- Blessings are crowning his head (Prov. 10:6)
- He speaks words of faith through love, growing in every way, more and more like Christ (Eph. 4:15)
- He is delivered from all his fears (Ps. 34:4)
- He continually worships the Lord (Ps. 34:1)
- His footsteps are ordered by the Lord and God directs his paths (Prov. 16:9)
- God's favor surrounds him as a shield (Ps. 5:12)

- Quietness and confidence shall be his strength (Is. 30:15)
- He is quick to hear, slow to speak, slow to anger (James 1:19)
- He loves the Lord with all his heart, mind, soul, and strength, and he loves his neighbor as himself (Matt. 22:37-39)
- He is devoting himself to lavishly supplementing his faith with goodness, and to goodness adding understanding, and to understanding adding the strength of self-control and patient endurance, and to patient endurance adding godliness and to godliness adding mercy toward his brothers and sisters, and to mercy toward others adding unending love (2 Peter 1:5-8 TPT)

God was teaching me to persevere, endure, and labor until I saw evidence of the power of His Word of Love begin to birth change in my husband. At times it really did seem as if I was giving birth. Birthing is difficult, painful and sometimes very long. I know from the experience of birthing my six children that the transition stage is the most difficult of all. Just before the moment of birth, it would seem that I would have no more strength. How many times did I cry out in travail, "I can't go on! I can't do this any longer!" But I would press on because the anticipation finally getting to see and hold my baby gave me the endurance and perseverance to press on.

The power of the Holy Spirit gave me strength. At times it was exhausting and discouraging and the enemy of my soul would try to convince me to give up, but Father God was teaching me to keep focused on the goal; the birth of newness and the miracles He was doing in my husband. I was pressing forward by His great grace and love strengthening me day to day—sometimes hour by hour—as I cried out to God! And I knew He was with me. There it is again, my favorite promise: "He will never leave me!" No matter how fierce the storm was, He was always there!

By His power and love He was reaching back into my husband's past and redeeming what had been lost to him, and healing his brokenness. I will never forget the day when he heard a preacher in our church telling us how much God loved us—and he believed it! Now it was not just in his head, but in his heart. He sat down in his favorite chair when we got home as if he were mesmerized by this wonderful truth that set him free. He kept saying, "God loves me! Wow! God loves me!" That truth set him free from anger. It was so remarkable! He would say, "Today I realized the abuse, neglect, and abandonment in my childhood had made me so *angry*. But God loves me, my Father in heaven loves me and He calls me His son!" That is what truth does; the truth sets us free! What an amazing Dad He is!

In the days and months that followed, God taught my husband how to worship and love Him. He laid his life upon the altar and was willing to allow the Lord to heal and restore his soul. He grew to love and cherish God's Word, and the words on the pages became life to him!

Somehow, God reached back into his past and brought healing and good out of the evil that was meant to destroy him. It was wonderful to experience what Father God did in him—He was a brand new man, a godly man—one who learned to love God, himself, and others! This is the true miracle: a changed life! Now God is using him to disciple other men who desire to be made whole and be set free.

God promised in His Word that He would give me double for my trouble. Isaiah 61:7 (NIV) says, "Instead of your shame you will receive a double portion, and instead of disgrace you will rejoice in your inheritance. And so you will inherit a double portion in your land, and everlasting joy will be yours." I asked God to do what He said He would do! And while I was waiting, God was stretching my faith in His Word as I was believing and relying on Him and growing more deeply in love with my Daddy God. He was changing my character, healing me, and building my faith as I trusted Him and experienced His endless love and acceptance of me, a joy and satisfaction like nothing I have ever known.

A Spirit of Honor

They refuse to slander or insult others; they'll never listen to gossip or rumors, nor would they ever harm another with their words (Psalm 15:3 TPT).

It seems that during the most difficult periods of my life is when God was changing me the most. I know it to be true. He is an incredible Daddy, turning something that was meant for my destruction into something good, beautiful, and lasting. When I was crying out and passionately seeking His love and presence every day and reading truth in His Love Book, then I was set free, knowing it was a privilege to experience His glorious love and be completely changed during the tumultuous years of my life.

The trials during this time seemed like they would destroy me. Some were a result of my own bad choices, and some were a result of my circumstances. They were loud, confusing, vociferous, and vehemently explosive—and seemed like a roller coaster of ups and downs designed to crush my faith. But His faithfulness was in the waiting. And daily I drew strength and expectation from hanging out with David in the Psalms. I was so thankful and privileged just to sit in the presence of God's love, approval, and acceptance. This is how I learned to be an overcomer. God taught me to overcome evil with good. He taught me to come against evil in the opposite spirit—the Spirit of His Son, and a spirit of honor, no matter what. He was teaching me how to love. As I read and meditated on this verse, I knew I could not slander my husband and gossip about him in prayer groups or to friends. God taught me and strengthened me by His Holy Spirit. When I read His Love Book, the spirit within me crashes into the truth. I knew God was telling me that it is very important to cover my husband, just like Jesus' blood covers my sins and He doesn't expose them to others. This is how it was with Noah:

> Noah, a man of the soil, proceeded to plant a vineyard. When he drank some of its wine, he became drunk and lay uncovered inside his tent. Ham, the father of Canaan, saw his father naked and told his two brothers outside. But Shem and Japheth took a robe, held it over their shoulders, and backed into the tent to cover their father. As they did this, they looked the other way so they would not see him naked (Gen. 9:20-23 NLT).

Father God's Word of Love taught me to honor and respect my husband; to "cover him" while His Good Father was healing and delivering him. I did not expose his nakedness to others. I covered him with a spirit of honor. I had made this marriage vow before God, a firm commitment.

> Marriage is the beautiful design of the Almighty, a great and sacred mystery—meant to be a vivid example of Christ and his church. So every married man should be gracious to his wife just as he is gracious to himself. And every wife should be tenderly devoted to her husband (Ephesians 5:32-33 TPT).

It was only by God's love and faithfulness to me and through the power and strength of His Spirit that I was full of courage and strength, believing in His Word that He would do what He said He would do.

> Even in times of trouble we have a joyful confidence, knowing that our pressures will develop in us patient endurance. And patient endurance will refine our character, and proven character leads us back to hope. And this hope is not a disappointing fantasy, because we can now experience the endless love of God cascading into our hearts through the Holy Spirit who lives in us! (Rom. 5:3-5 TPT).

Our struggles are meant to bring out our true beauty. Just as a butterfly begins to struggle its way out of a cocoon to become something beautiful, so our struggles are meant to bring out our true beauty. If one were to help a butterfly end its struggling and free it of its cocoon, it would die. The same analogy applies to the struggles that we have in our life in Christ, they are tailor-made for each individual. The Great Master knows exactly the right moment when the struggle has accomplished what it was set out to do—and only then will He set you free, allowing the beautiful man or woman of God to emerge through His endless love.

We Can't Change Our Husbands, or Can We?

All of us know that we can't change another person, so why do we keep on trying? When we hear these words, "you can't change your husband," our mind automatically thinks of this statement in a negative way. I have had many women ask me what they can do to change their husbands to become the spiritual leader in their homes the way that God has intended for a marriage to function.

Let's start out by **what not to do:**

- Do not leave a book open by his chair that instructs men on how to be the leader in their homes.
- Do not play praise and worship music as loud as you can or change the channel in the car to the Christian station from where he had it set.
- Do not talk loudly on the phone to your friends about how disappointed you are in this part of your marriage.
- Most importantly: **DO NOT NAG HIM!**

CAUTION:

Now let's look at what the Bible says about how you might really change your husband. I caution you not to read on if you're really not sincere about seeing him changed.

I Peter 3 instructs wives to be devoted to their husbands so that even if some of them don't obey the Word (loving their wives as Christ loves the church), they will be won over and the wife won't even have to say a thing. A simple definition of the word *devoted* is "very loving" or "loyal." So Peter is telling us if you love your husband you can change him. (See the biblical definition of love in I Corinthians 13.) Does it take time? Absolutely! But what is Father God accomplishing in this whole process? *We* are being changed as well. The most impacting scripture for me in I Peter chapter 3 talks about how Sarah devoted herself (was very loving and loyal) to her husband, Abraham, and that we will be her daughters if we do not fear.

I remember meditating on that for some time. What does this scripture mean? We will be her daughters if we do not fear. Fear what? Giving up of our own desires, giving up control? Fearing that our finances will crumble if we allow our husband to lead in this area? Fear that our wants and desires will not be met? Fear if we love our husband so devotedly he will not love us back? The most important thing we can do is to learn to love.

I can honestly say this is the number one scripture that has increased my faith and my intimate relationship with Father God more than any other passage! By putting this verse into action, I totally had to trust my Papa! My hope was in Him because when you really take a look at this one verse, it's a promise! When I loved and was gentle, kind, forgiving, and I humbled myself, I kept a tight hold on that anchor; and I reminded God that if I did not fear, I would be a daughter of Sarah. I love how *The Passion Translation* puts Hebrews 11:11: "For the authority of her faith rested in the One who made the promise, and she tapped into his faithfulness." We can tap into God's faithfulness, and rest in His promise, just like Sarah did.

Did I mess up? Absolutely! And if you study the life of Sarah, you will find that she made mistakes too. But we have a forgiving, merciful God who will pick us back up and teach us and guide us. I purposed in my heart that I would also be a woman of strong faith like Sarah—no matter what I faced. My faith and trust were in my God and His Word, not in my husband.

So it is true, we can change our husbands, *by loving them* and trusting God and His faithfulness—and in the process you will probably be changed more than they are.

And while He was refining my faith and my character, *His faithfulness was in the waiting.*

Chapter 4: Surrounded

"I love you [fervently and devotedly], O Lord, my strength."
The Lord is my rock, my fortress, and the One who rescues
me; my God, my rock and strength in whom I trust and take
refuge; My shield, and the horn of my salvation, my high
tower—my stronghold. I call upon the Lord, who is worthy
to be praised; and I am saved from my enemies. The cords
of death surrounded me, and the streams of ungodliness
and torrents of destruction terrified me. The cords of Sheol
(the nether world, the place of the dead) surrounded me; the
snares of death confronted me. In my distress [when I seemed
surrounded] I called upon the Lord and cried to my God for
help; He heard my voice from His temple, And my cry for help
came before Him, into His very ears (Psalm 18:1-6 AMP).

Desperation

Can you hear the cries of David in this psalm? Saul's army had
surrounded David and was getting ready to kill him. He was
desperate as he cried out to God. Just like David, sometimes I
find myself surrounded by desperation; desperate to be loved, approved of,
and accepted. It's like being in a prison bound by loneliness, depression,
rejection, abandonment, fear, shame, and guilt. How does this happen?
I feel like I'm in a combat zone, fighting for my freedom. One minute
I'm stable and secure, and the next minute I'm attacked with thoughts of
worthlessness and hopelessness. I put a smile on my face and pretend all is

well because I have to be strong. Someone told me I have to be strong—strong for my husband and children—but I am broken and trapped on the inside. I feel like a prisoner of war in my own mind. The battle is fierce and I wonder how I can be free? So I start to cry out to God as David did because I was surrounded by my enemy.

What Is the Most Important Thing You Need in Your Life?

I was in a worship service one morning enjoying the songs and coming into God's presence when I heard the Spirit ask me, "What is the most important thing you need in your life?" I wasn't sure how to answer that, so I was truthful when I replied, "I'm not sure, Lord." He said, "A Father. That is the most important thing you have needed in your life." And I knew that Daddy God was telling me that He was waiting for me to know Him as my Father. He is always faithful, waiting for me to pursue a relationship with Him—and I knew this would be the freedom from my desperation.

I wish I could say it was easy, fast, and uncomplicated—but it wasn't. I read blogs, I read books. I listened to my friend's advice. But it was in a morning worship service in a small country church when God answered me. That's when I began to know Him as my Daddy. This is how my freedom was to come—by knowing and believing His love for me. Just sitting quietly in the Lord's presence, listening for His voice just as a child waits for her daddy to come home after he's been gone on a trip. I was waiting for my Daddy, for His presence and love to surround me in His big arms.

Did it take time? Yes, it took time. I woke up early every morning, knowing He was waiting for me. Relationships always take time to develop. But I was desperate to have an intimate relationship with God and I wanted to be healed and free. Did it take time to break those strongholds in my life? Absolutely! Now that I look back, I think it was because my Daddy wanted to spend time with ME! I just have to tell everyone how much I love my Daddy, and declare as David did in Psalm 18:1: "I love you O Lord, my strength!" Psalm 18 is my favorite Psalm. (But I say that about each one!) It's the psalm of David's life and how God rescued him and how intimately he came to know his Father God. I knew if David could know God intimately, then so could I. "I love you, O Lord, my strength!" This is my declaration of freedom!

A Beautiful Life: Total Make Over, a Brand New Me

> Stop imitating the ideals and opinions of the culture around you, but be inwardly transformed by the Holy Spirit through a total reformation of how you think. This will empower you to discern God's will as you live a beautiful life, satisfying and perfect in his eyes (Romans 12:2 TPT).

We need to have a reformation in how we think. Wrong thinking says "I am not worthy," and is always looking for man's approval, crying out for acceptance. When our thinking isn't changed our past follows us everywhere, telling us that we are not loved and that there's no hope for us after what we've done. When others exclude us (many times not even trying to be mean to us) it is that same dreaded feeling of rejection; the same feeling I had as a little girl when I wasn't picked for the kickball game or when I wasn't invited to the birthday party. We get so fearful that anxiety and worry keep us up at night. The hurtful words of others come back to haunt us, telling us that we are failures. On and on those thoughts parade their way through our mind, thoughts about the person we used to be—and that is how strongholds are established in the mind. But can it really be as easy as changing the way we think? Is it simple?

Somehow when my marital issues began, I wasn't able to see God's perspective from His Love Book—how He sees me—because I was so caught up in my own emotional hurts. I wasn't always in love with His Word until a friend told me that His Word is so powerful that it could change my life, and that the truth in God's Love Book would set me free. Then slowly and steadily, the Spirit would lead me to the truth that began to change my thinking. My Daddy God said to me, "See, Pearl, it is the truth that you **know** that sets you free"(John 8:32).

Clothed with Strength and Dignity

It was like putting on a whole new wardrobe—changed from the inside out. I remember reading in Proverbs 31 that I am clothed with strength and dignity. As a woman, I chuckled to myself because it was like wearing undergarments that were old and raggedy and full of holes and putting a beautiful, brand new dress over them. In your mind, you don't really feel beautiful in your gorgeous dress, pearls, and new shoes because you know what's underneath. Nobody else saw the raggedy old undergarments—but I knew they were there. I didn't really feel beautiful. I might have looked like I had it all together on the outside, but I knew all the raggedy, old stuff that still remained on the inside; thoughts that kept me insecure and full of fear. This is how I related to this truth that was to be mine, "I am clothed with strength and dignity." That was the beginning of the truth that was to set me free. Every time a thought would come into my mind that said, "I'm not worthy," or "I'll never amount to anything." I changed my thinking with, "I am a woman of God and I am clothed with strength and dignity." This truth began to develop a quiet confidence in me and I began to believe that I was beautiful on the inside and the outside. I am so amazed at my Abba Daddy when I look back through His Word and realize how much it has changed me from the inside out!

I began pulling down those thoughts which had such a strong hold on me, and instead I believed that I was surrounded by God's unrelenting grip— just like a dad's big strong arms around His daughter. I quickly learned that where my thoughts go, my life follows. Changing my thinking changed my life. I began to pursue and love God's Word as if my life depended on it—*because it does!*

> So here's what I want you to do, God helping you: Take your everyday, ordinary life—your sleeping, eating, going-to-work, and walking-around life—and place it before God as an offering. Embracing what God does for you is the best thing you can do for him. Don't become so well-adjusted to your culture that you fit into it without even thinking.

Instead, fix your attention on God. You'll be changed from the inside out. Readily recognize what he wants from you, and quickly respond to it. Unlike the culture around you, always dragging you down to its level of immaturity, God brings the best out of you, develops well-formed maturity in you (Romans 12:1-2 MSG).

Freedom from Remembering So I Can Go on Living

I remember when the Lord spoke gently to me about forgiveness. It is so remarkable to me that when God speaks to me, I can remember exactly where I was and what I was doing. On this specific day I was cleaning the bathroom (my every day, ordinary life), and a thought came to me about something hurtful that my husband had said to me. Immediately, God asked me, "Can you forgive him?" I swallowed hard and wondered how I could answer anything but yes to the One who had forgiven all my sins. Out of reverence for God, I answered, "Yes, Lord." Then He asked me another question, "In fact, my Precious Pearl, every time you have a thought about unkind things that your husband has said, will you forgive him?" And I answered yes again. Every time I would have a memory, I would speak to myself and say, "But I forgive him." I didn't understand or realize how much this promise to my Daddy God would transform so many areas of my life. Here are some of the ways that it changed me:

1. I learned how to forgive. I learned in His Word that if I did not forgive I would still be held prisoner in my own mind and I would not live my life to the fullest that Jesus died for me to have.

2. I learned how to renew my mind. I did this by taking every thought captive and by keeping my promise to God. I had to think about what I was thinking about and not just let my mind wander anywhere it wanted to go.

We demolish arguments and every pretension that sets itself up against the knowledge of God, and we take captive every thought to make it obedient to Christ (2 Cor. 10:5 NIV).

3. I was actually forgetting the past and looking forward to what was in my future. This was the most miraculous thing that happened to me. I never thought that it would be possible to forget all the angry words, moments, and scenes that would play over and over in my mind. I can't recall one time that my husband's anger towards me was out of control. Not one! I was being made just like my Daddy God, just like Hebrews 8:12 says (NLT): "And I will forgive their wickedness, and I will never again remember their sins."

I was forgiving my husband and at the same time I was forgetting and being made new—transformed. This seemed impossible, but with my Dad all things are possible! It was the beginning of how I learned to renew my mind. I was experiencing the Word at work in my life and how to believe it and take it by faith.

What Women Really Want

I have returned again and again to this psalm. It has breathed over me like a gentle song, and it lingers in my mind. It has brought me back again and again; this verse especially has brought me to closer faith and trust and intimacy with my God:

"Thy gentleness has made me great" (Psalm 18:35 KJV).

I asked a group of women what they *really* want in a man. Overwhelmingly, the first item on the list was a godly man who will lead with confidence and strength. And the second, most popular answer was gentleness. It seems like an oxymoron, doesn't it? Strong, but gentle. But this is God himself, isn't it? I had to learn this because I thought that God was angry and punished me when I did something wrong. But as I poured over the scriptures I learned my God was gentle! Those tender words washed over me as I drank the words in from Isaiah that He gathers the lambs in his arms and carries them close to his heart, *gently* leading them. In another passage, Paul tells Timothy to make sure he chooses elders wisely. He tells him one of the qualifications must be that they are not violent, but *gentle.*

Women want men who will lead with strength; men who will protect and provide, but treat them with gentleness. Paul even tells Timothy to pursue gentleness—to go after it! Paul explained that it will make him great and it is a sure mark of a secure man, one who doesn't use his strength to be overbearing and unkind. Every woman wants a secure man who is strong, but gentle.

I have learned that my Papa is gentleness—in every sense of the word, that is who He is to me. Jesus himself said that He is gentle and lowly in heart. (See Matt. 11:29.)

So when this verse says, "His gentleness has made me great," it just might be worth it, husbands, to pursue this virtue because it's what every woman wants!

Just Give it to God: How Do You Do That?

One evening I was teaching a series at a woman's meeting about the story of Rachel and Leah from Genesis 29:13-35 and Genesis 30:1-22. Jacob had made an agreement with Laban that he would work for him for seven years for his youngest daughter, Rachel.

> Now Laban had two daughters, Leah was the older and Rachel the younger. Leah had weak eyes, but Rachel was stunningly beautiful. And it was Rachel that Jacob loved. So Jacob answered, "I will work for you seven years for your younger daughter Rachel." But Laban tricked Jacob and brought Leah to the marriage bed because she was the oldest daughter and it was customary that the oldest daughter married first. Jacob woke up the next morning and discovered it was Leah and not Rachel. Laban had tricked him. But Laban told him complete your honeymoon week

with Leah and I will give you Rachel but you will have to work another seven years for me...Jacob made love to Rachel also, and his love for Rachel was greater than his love for Leah" The story goes on to describe how desperately Leah wanted to be loved...Leah became pregnant and gave birth to a son. She named him Reuben, for she said, "It is because the Lord has seen my misery. Surely my husband will love me now." (Gen. 29:16-18, 30, 29, my paraphrase).

That night I was specifically teaching about how devastating it must have been for Leah—the rejection, unworthiness, and the sheer desperation of wanting to be loved by her husband. I was sharing my personal story of the pain and rejection that I had experienced in my own life and how I desperately wanted to be loved unconditionally. I also shared how this proved to be a gift to me, and how I poured over the Psalms and would listen when Holy Spirit spoke to me about how Father God saw my anguish and would set me free, just like in this scripture:

I will be glad and rejoice in your love, for you saw my affliction and knew the anguish of my soul (Psalm 31:7).

However, Rachel also was desperate for something. She was barren. She could not have children, and by this time her sister, Leah, had given Jacob four sons.

When Rachel saw that she conceived no children for Jacob, she envied her sister, and said to Jacob, "Give me children, or else I will die." Then Jacob became furious with Rachel, and he said, "Am I in the place of God, who has denied you children?" (Gen. 30:1-2 AMP).

Rachel's desire to have children had now turned into desperation, and that desperation turned into jealousy. Jealousy is a very dangerous stronghold and it causes us to be barren—unfruitful—because jealousy begins by using comparisons. God's Word is very wise when it tells us not to compare ourselves with one another. Jealousy will cause us to be controlling and manipulative in order to get what we want. The root of jealousy is insecurity. I had to find out who I was in Christ, what He said about me in His Word, and then that quiet confidence of knowing who I was began shutting down the voice in my head that said I wasn't worthy. We will always act like what we think we are. Begin speaking over your life that you are clothed with strength and dignity. No more raggedy undergarments! Shut down the voices in your mind, and the truth will set you free.

My own desperation to be loved was a cry to know my Father's love. If He had left me alone, I would not have known love. Desperation produces strongholds, which produce barrenness and bitterness. It was His Word and the presence of His love that satisfied my cry to be loved. Now I know I can trust my Daddy God to guard all of my desires and that He will break the strongholds in my life.

There are so many strongholds that form in our minds. If we believe we are not loved, that we are not worthy, or accepted, then that is where the battle is—in our minds. Sometimes we convince ourselves that if a certain person would just love us—mother, father, husband, wife, sister, daughter, etc.—then the anguish would stop. It is our responsibility to prevent these strongholds from taking root in our minds.

> In my distress I called to the Lord; I cried to my God for help. From his temple he heard my voice; my cry came before him, into his ears. (Psalm 18:6).

If David cried out to God, then so can I. And if God listened to David, He will listen to me. I didn't see immediate change, but God was giving me eagle's wings, renewing my strength, and teaching me to walk by faith and intimacy with my Abba Daddy. My value, strength, and dignity are in Him along with my happiness, fulfillment, and joy. No other person can fulfill that in my life!

> He satisfies [my] desires with good things so that [my] youth is renewed like the eagle's (Psalm 103:5, changes mine).

These were the truths that I taught about on the first night of the seminar. I began packing up my Bible and papers when a woman approached me and told me briefly about her struggle in her marriage and how distraught she was. My answer to her was, "Just give it to God." I heard myself saying that, and I cringed at my own words—how many times had a well-meaning Christian woman flippantly said that to me, leaving me in my hopelessness and despair—left to find my own way out of desperation. I realized I had just done the same thing to this beautiful woman of God as she stared down at the floor and said, "I don't know how to do that."

As I drove home that night, this woman who believed she was in a hopeless situation was on my mind, and I was determined with God's help and the truth of His Word to teach her "how to give it to God." How often do we carelessly give a pat answer as insincere advice to people who need help because they believe they are in an impossible situation. I knew sometimes the reason God allows us to go through some tough situations is to help those that are going through the same thing.

> Praise be to the God and Father of our Lord Jesus Christ, the Father of compassion and the God of all comfort, who comforts us in all our troubles, so that we can comfort those in any trouble with the comfort we ourselves receive from God, for just as we share abundantly in the sufferings of Christ, so also our comfort abounds through Christ (2 Cor. 1:3-5).

I wanted to tell this woman and many others that they could find comfort in my Daddy God. How many times have I quietly sat in His lap with my head on His chest and He eased my distress. He spoke through His Love Book and taught me how to change my life by changing my thinking. I knew I must pray and seek Him for answers for this woman, not some theological book knowledge, but practically, how to "cast her cares" upon God. This is the tactic of the enemy: to get us so focused on anxiety and worry that we become discouraged and depressed, then he comes in for what he is really trying to steal—our hope! If he's got our hope, he's got our dreams; if he's got our dreams, he has our future.

But as I sat down at my computer that week, I realized that the task wasn't that easy. I knew my freedom had come from spending time with God and hanging out with David in the Psalms. I was saying to the Lord, "What do You want me to tell her? How do you teach intimacy in a relationship?" The Lord had been teaching me to walk by faith and intimacy with Him, that my value and dignity come from Him, and that my happiness, fulfillment, and joy are satisfied only in Him. His Word and the power of His Spirit healed my soul.

The Psalms express the emotion of the writer to God and his gratitude for rescuing him every time. David cried out to the Lord continually and knew God loved him so much that He would rescue him every time.

> He led me to a place of safety; he rescued me because he delights in me" (Psalm 18:19 NLT).

God placed the Psalms right in the center of the Bible—right in the heart of all the other books. As I read the Psalms day after day and month after month, I began experiencing the healing balm of the Father's love. I heard the whisper of His voice as He answered me, "Tell her that I love her."

Tell Them That I Love Them

I remember the first step to my healing and intimate relationship with Father God was that I believed that He loved me, and there was nothing I could do that would stop Him from loving me! He instructed me to say it out loud every day, even to look in the mirror and say, "God loves me!" I did this until I began to believe it, and this was the early training for renewing my mind and changing the way I think. What freedom! To know that I am loved and I finally have a Dad! It was wonderful to know in my mind and heart the love that is steadfast and unchanging—this extravagant love that comforts me and has been poured into me through His Holy Spirit. Unconditional love—finally!

I had a revelation that He loved me for me. And I knew this in my heart, not just in my mind.

I began to pray the prayer that Paul prayed in Ephesians over myself every day:

> "So I kneel humbly in awe before the Father of our Lord Jesus, the Messiah, the perfect Father of every father and child in heaven and on the earth. And I pray that he would unveil within me the unlimited riches of his glory and favor until supernatural strength floods my innermost being with his divine might and explosive power. Then, by constantly using my faith, the life of Christ will be released deep inside me, and the resting place of his love will become the very source and root of my life. Then I will be empowered to discover what every holy one experiences—the great magnitude of the astonishing love of Christ in all its dimensions. How deeply intimate and far-reaching is his love! How enduring and inclusive it is! Endless love beyond measurement that transcends our understanding—this extravagant love pours into you until you are filled to overflowing with the fullness of God!" (Adapted from Ephesians 3:14-19 TPT.)

The following week I shared with the women that love is where we must always begin in God. His love is limitless, and this is how we begin to know Him. I told them what I did to break through the barriers in my mind and at last believe the Father's total unconditional affection for me. It's a transition; it takes time and faith to believe that His love is real. I reminded them that we are imperfect women, perfectly loved. We can't earn His love; we can only receive His love. As I spoke, I could see tears well up in their eyes as I spoke about the unconditional love that these women and many others have been longing for. Nothing else will satisfy. I heard audible sighs as if some women were so grateful that they didn't have to *do* anything, they couldn't be good enough or perfect enough. We prayed a simple prayer to get them going on this journey of freedom of striving and looking for love: "Father God, please help me to receive Your love and know in the deepest part of my being that You love me. Amen."

I found the answer to my question, "Father God, how do I teach intimacy?" I can't. A deep, loving, intimate relationship must be experienced. *His faithfulness is in the waiting.*

Chapter 5: Destroying Fortresses

After giving these women instructions for their week for how to pray and receive the Father's love and believe that He loved them, I began to give them tools and guidelines for "how to give it to God." That is what they are: just tools and guidelines, and my own miraculous transformation testimony. It is simple, but hard; we have to change our thinking about relationships so we no longer have to prove our worth and strive to earn the love and affection of others.

After praying and reading and listening, I knew God wanted me to continue to teach on the way we think because this is the key that will change our life, and is one of the steps to breaking strongholds in our minds.

One of the first things I have always practiced is sitting down with Daddy God—purposefully making time to sit and tell Him exactly how I feel and what's going on in my life. I know He will always help me, because that's what Dads do. This is a very crucial step and cannot be skipped. This is what relationship is all about—spending time with Him, being honest, and pouring everything out as I sit at His feet. If David did, then so can I, and become "a woman after God's heart." Listen to how David pours out his heart to the Lord:

> O God of my life, I'm lovesick for you in this weary wilderness. I thirst with the deepest longings to love you more, with cravings in my heart that can't be described. Such yearning grips my soul for you, my God! I'm energized every time I enter your heavenly sanctuary to seek more

of your power and drink in more of your glory. For your tender mercies mean more to me than life itself. How I love and praise you, God! Daily I will worship you passionately with all my heart. My arms will wave to you like banners of praise. I overflow with praise when I come before you, for the anointing of your presence satisfies me like nothing else. You are such a rich banquet of pleasure to my soul. I lie awake each night thinking of you and reflecting on how you help me like a father. I sing through the night under your splendor-shadow, offering up to you my songs of delight and joy! With passion I pursue and cling to you. Because I feel your grip on my life, I keep my soul close to your heart (Psalm 63:1-8 TPT).

I love how David says, "I keep my soul close to your heart." Heart to heart. I literally picture myself being washed by the Father's love and waiting for His wisdom and council. On this particular day as I prayed and asked God how I should continue this teaching about changing our thinking and tearing down strongholds in our lives, He led me through His Word (which is one thing the Holy Spirit does—He leads and guides us in truth).

Make No Mistake about It, We Are in a War

First of all let's be clear about what a stronghold is. I understood the word *stronghold* much better when I broke it down into two words: strong hold. So simply put, it is when something has a strong hold on you. In the physical sense, picture a wrestling match where one opponent has a strong hold on the other.

Ironically enough, spiritually speaking, we are the ones who put a strong hold on ourselves! We build strongholds in our minds by a habitual pattern of thinking. So a *stronghold* can be defined as a habitual pattern of thought that is built into our tminds. Do you see why I am so emphatic about changing our thinking and believing what God says about us?

Remember the story of Leah and Rachel in the previous chapter? Leah desperately wanted to be loved by her husband; her stronghold was rejection. Rachel desperately wanted to have a child; her stronghold was jealousy. More examples of strongholds are depression, need for approval, discouragement, shame, guilt, anger, complaining, fear, unforgiveness, bitterness, abandonment, and worry.

That week in the women's seminar I continued the teaching with the scripture below, which is key for breaking strongholds in our lives and living a life of blessing and freedom:

> For though we live in the world we do not **wage war** as the world does. The **weapons** we **fight** with are not the weapons of the world. On the contrary, they have divine **power** to **demolish strongholds**, we demolish arguments and every pretension that sets itself up against the knowledge of God, and we **take captive** every thought to make it obedient to Christ (2 Cor. 10:3-5).

Note that the words that I highlighted are military terms:

- Wage war
- Weapons
- Fight
- Demolish
- Strongholds
- Take captive

Do you see how the strongholds in this verse clearly refer to our way of thinking, and are lies that are contrary to the Word of God? Strongholds are hard to remove unless a concentrated effort is made to remove them. They have been so engrained into our thinking that they can be described metaphorically as a fortress. A fortress is an armed stronghold, which is normally a greatly fortified town containing a large military base. It can also be referred to as a castle, a fort, tower, or a bunker. Wow! That's a person who has their "walls up"! We have all known people like that. Do you have walls up? I certainly did—I had a whole city living in my thoughts!

We live our lives according to these thinking patterns. Values, feelings, attitudes, moods, and our actions come out of these wrong thinking patterns. Some of these strongholds have been part of our thinking since childhood, and may take some time to destroy them.

But Paul says in that verse that it is **possible** to take every thought captive to make it obedient to Christ. In our meeting we broke this verse down starting with, "We do not wage war as the world does." What might the world use to "wage war"? Here are some examples the women came up with:

- Isolation: Isolating yourself if you are feeling depressed/discouraged

- Give into addictions: Alcohol, food, drugs, shopping

- Taking offense: Stop talking to "them"

- Gossip/slander: Posting it on social media, texting

- Anger/retaliation: Just tell them what you think

The next part of this verse says, "The weapons we fight with are not weapons of the world." What are our spiritual weapons? Here are eleven different spiritual weapons that we have as believers.

1. Recognize the enemy! This first point is extremely important, and I can't stress it enough. We do not wage war against people—*ever!* Eph. 6:12 says, "For our struggle is not against flesh and blood, but against the rulers, against the authorities, against the powers of this dark world and against the spiritual forces of evil in the heavenly realms."

2. Put your armor on! See Eph. 6:13-17.

3. Read the Word of God daily.

4. Have faith. Receive and believe what the Word says.

5. Use the name of Jesus and the blood of Jesus.

6. Pray.

7. Exercise forgiveness. Always forgive quickly, yourself and others.

8. Declare and decree the Word.

9. Spend time developing intimacy with God in His presence.

10. Worship Him.

11. Surround yourself with other believers. Attend church; your closest friends should be believers.

The third part of the verse which says, "Take every thought captive" may seem impossible, but it is extremely important. Practically speaking, how do we do this? First and foremost, we ask the Holy Spirit to help us. Just pray a simple prayer like this one: "Holy Spirit, I need your help today, and I give you permission to let me know immediately when I'm thinking wrong thoughts so I can cast them down into the ground where they will have no effect on me." Simply put: *pay attention to what you are thinking about!* Develop selective thinking.

I previously shared that every time I would think about something my husband had said to me I used my weapon of forgiveness. I would combat that negative thought by saying, "No! I do not receive that thought anymore; I forgive him." Eventually I had not only forgiven him, but I had forgotten as well—that is powerful and that is called freedom!

Change your thinking, change your life!

Live in the blessing of God as you meditate on this scripture:

> Stop imitating the ideals and opinions of the culture around you, but be inwardly transformed by the Holy Spirit through a total reformation of *how you think*. This will empower you to discern God's will as you live a beautiful life, satisfying and perfect in his eyes (Rom. 12:2 TPT).

51

Take No Thought

Let's look at this in another way from Jesus' teaching in Matthew 6:24-34 (KJV). Jesus says "take no thought" five times. *Take* means to receive. Do you see that? We do not have to "take" (receive) every thought that comes into our mind! Jesus was saying to stop worrying about yourself. Take every thought captive until you tear the fortress down in your mind. Ask Holy Spirit to help you by saying something like: "If I'm thinking incorrectly about _____, and if I have built a stronghold in my mind, please expose it so I can cooperate with You and tear it down." Remember, this will help you live a beautiful, peaceful, and satisfying life.

As a checklist for my thoughts (as I think about what I'm thinking about), I use Phil. 4:8. I ask, "Is this thought true, noble, right, pure, lovely, admirable, excellent, and praiseworthy?" When a thought comes, you can either accept it or reject it. Just like an umpire, it's either in or it's out. Remember, this is very important: when we take (receive) a thought, it becomes a pattern of our thinking.

Thoughts become attitudes, and attitudes become moods if we do not capture that first thought. We all have experienced someone walking into a room and we can "feel" their mood. When this happens to you, everybody knows your stuff. Don't let that be you!

Give it to God!

The Word says, "Cast all your anxiety on him because he cares for you" (I Peter 5:7). *Cast* is a strong word, it refers to throwing something down forcefully. Some examples of *cares* are anxiety, worry, wrong desires, and discontentment. Cares come and choke the Word out of our lives (just like weeds in a garden) and we can't enjoy the intimacy with our Beloved Father.

We need to immediately cast our cares on the Lord. To do this, tell Father God, "I will believe and agree with what Your Word says about this. I roll this over on You now, and I will only believe what You say. Holy Spirit, I need Your help to apply this to my life." And if the same thought comes back again, just repeat this prayer.

When I was praying and asking the Lord how to teach this woman at the seminar to "cast her care on the Lord" this is what He had me do. I brought an ash bucket from my fireplace and some note cards and I instructed the women to:

1. Write down any care, anxieties, or worries that have been troubling them.

2. Place them in the ash bucket and pray and tell Jesus you're giving them to Him. There were many tears shed and hugs and much comfort among the women.

3. I told them that I will burn all their "cares" in my fireplace.

4. The following week I had tucked some of the ashes in envelopes and the women put the envelopes in their Bibles to remind them that they had cast their cares on Jesus and that He gives us beauty for ashes (see Is. 61:1-3).

This has been my basic training as I have learned to fight this battle in my mind. If I can do it, so can you! I take any memories that have hurt me—taking each one as the enemy tried to remind me of it—and I spoke to myself, *loudly* and forcefully, and cast that thought down, saying, "No; I choose to forgive!" I put the truth of the Word on those thoughts, time and time again. Why? Because I made a promise to my Abba Daddy that I would forgive!

Let's take a look at another scripture that can help us wage war against worry and anxiety:

> Do not be anxious (worry) about anything, but in every situation, by prayer and petition, with thanksgiving, present your requests to God. And the peace of God, which transcends all understanding, will guard your hearts and your minds in Christ Jesus (Philippians 4:6-7, additions mine).

All of us have struggled with this peace stealer: anxiety (worry). This scripture has been life-changing for me. This is a passage worth memorizing and putting in your arsenal to defeat the enemy who comes to steal, kill, and destroy. One of the things he wants to steal is our peace, but Paul gives us specific instructions about this:

First: Pray. No matter what is worrying you, pray!

Secondly: Be thankful. This is the key that has combated many thoughts for me. When I can't seem to pull that anxious thought down, I start being thankful. If I'm in my home or driving my car, wherever I am, I start thanking Him for everything I can think of. This is really an amazing weapon because thankfulness is part of our faith walk. Begin to put this in to practice, and you will experience the supernatural peace of God (Do you see that in that scripture?) Thankfulness will *guard our hearts and minds* with His peace! I cannot stress how effective this weapon is, this weapon of thankfulness. It's very simple, but very powerful. Sometimes you might have to actually speak it out loud because when we speak, it interrupts our thoughts and we let the enemy know, "I trust my God; I don't see the answer yet, but I trust my God!"

Taking every thought captive may seem like an insurmountable task, but Holy Spirit gives us power for the impossible. We take one thought at a time—one step at a time—whenever we learn anything new. This is extremely instrumental in learning to hear the voice of the Holy Spirit as His plan and purpose begins to unfold in our lives.

Man's approval or God's?

> Lord, you know everything there is to know about me. You perceive every movement of my heart and soul, and you understand my every thought before it even enters my mind. You are so intimately aware of me, Lord. You read my heart like an open book and you know all the words I'm about to speak before I even start a sentence!

You know every step I will take before my journey even begins (Psalm 139:1-4 TPT).

On the last night of the seminar I shared my personal experience of breaking strongholds in my own life:

It happened on an ordinary day in my ordinary life. Funny how I can remember where I was and what I was doing when my Daddy speaks to me. I was making lasagna in my kitchen for the guests we were having for dinner that evening. Romans talks about this:

> Take your everyday, ordinary life—your sleeping, eating, going-to-work and walking-around life—and place it before God as an offering (Rom. 12:1 MSG).

I was listening to a teaching while I was cooking, and something the woman said on the CD caught my attention as I was adding the garlic to my sauce. I started stirring the sauce and something told me to rewind and listen to that part again. She was talking about how God created every human being with a need for acceptance and approval, and how ultimately when we accept Christ as our Lord and Savior, that need is satisfied.

This came at a time in my life when a close family member was not speaking to me. I had tried calling her and leaving her messages, begging her to meet with me so we could talk, but to no avail. I was heartbroken, and this was all I could seem to think about! I would pray, I would cast my care, and give it to Jesus. I was grieving for this relationship, and the enemy seemed to be tormenting my mind. There seemed to be no hope of reconciliation with this woman who I had grown to love so deeply. I often thought of Psalm 55 when David said, "If an enemy were insulting me, I could endure it; if a foe were rising against me, I could hide. But it is you, a man like myself, my companion, my close friend, with whom I once enjoyed sweet fellowship at the house of God, as we walked among the worshipers."

I related so much to David; it would be so much easier if it was an enemy, a critic—but it was my best friend! I kept crying out to God, certain I could not endure another day of this despair if He did not fix it. *I just wanted him to fix it!*

Day after day, week after week, this played out in my mind. As I pressed the rewind button on the CD, I put down my wooden spoon, and with undivided attention I listened again because I knew my Abba Daddy was speaking through this Bible teacher directly to me. It is so awesome how Holy Spirit does that! She was saying that if we were looking for acceptance or approval from another person, this will become a stronghold in our lives. I knew at that moment I had allowed a stronghold to form in my mind for the need of acceptance from this person. I remember thinking that *stronghold* was the most appropriate word for this kind of thinking because it has a strong hold on you, so much that it forms a pattern of thinking in your mind that is deceptive and can consume your life. This had so much molded itself into my thinking that I was sure I could not be happy unless this relationship was restored.

The woman on the CD went on to say that the first thing someone needs to do in order to break a stronghold is to repent. I immediately turned the stove off, stopped stirring my sauce, and sat down to ask God to forgive me for desiring acceptance and approval from this person instead of Him. I began weeping, as I forgave her for wounding me, and I had to forgive myself for allowing this to continue for so long.

I really can't put it into words, but the most amazing thing happened: I felt a weight being lifted off of my shoulders and I knew I had broken the stronghold! Up until this point I did not know you could break strongholds in your own life. I thought someone who was very anointed would have to pray over you. But on that day, Holy Spirit was teaching me that I could do it myself—beginning with forgiveness and repentance. I committed myself to trust my Abba to satisfy my desires. I began declaring Psalm 103:5 and inserting my name into it, "God satisfies my desires with good things, my youth is renewed like the eagle's." I put on my "eagles wings" and I was free! I found a long-lasting satisfying love—I was accepted and approved! He is the every moment of my every day, ordinary life. He makes me more than I can be!

Remember also, beloved ones, we must be on guard when Satan tries to accuse us again and again and we have to remind him (out loud) that we have repented and received forgiveness with the blood of the Lamb as our defense!

Keys to Breaking Spiritual Strongholds

So based on what the Holy Spirit has taught me over the years, here are some keys for breaking strongholds off of your life:

- Repent and ask for forgiveness.

- Forgive anyone who has hurt you, and also forgive yourself. (Also, ask forgiveness from anyone you have hurt.)

- Commit to meeting with our Beloved Father every day. Set an appointment with God and keep it. Set the time and the place. Commit to trusting God, and receive His mercy. Remember, He is the only one who can change you! Receive daily doses of the Word; this will increase your faith. Send text messages with scriptures to yourself. Download an audio Bible app to your phone or tablet. This will break the patterns of your thinking. Remember: *change your thinking, change your life!*

- Believe you are loved by God. Tell yourself, "I am His and He is mine. He is my beloved and I am His. He takes great delight in me!"

- Be still and listen for His voice to speak to you. Sometimes you hear Him through the Word, and sometimes you hear Him in your heart.

- Write down what he says to you, either from His Word or in your heart. This is so important because we easily forget what He speaks to us. This has kept me focused on how He is changing me. I see progression in my journals from being selfish and self-centered to desiring righteousness and holiness. When I read my journals, it almost takes on the persona of being in a counselor's office. I reflect on how The Lord has changed me, the way I think, the way I feel, and what I desire and what I do. I am filled with gratitude and love and devotion when I read how He loved me in my brokenness and healed me. It is remarkable when I read this journey with Him how He has delivered me from all my fears and how I trust Him because He has promised to never leave me, and how I now believe He is faithful. I get so much satisfaction from reading how it used to be "all about me," and how this slow and steady walk of faith is producing fruit that will glorify my God; my God who has been so faithful in the waiting!

- Sit in His presence, experience His love, and thank Him for setting you free!

- When your strongholds have been broken, believe in faith that Abba Father will pay you back double for whatever you have lost. This is promised to us in His Word:

> Return to your Stronghold, O prisoners of hope; today I declare that I will restore to you double (Zech. 9:12 ESV).

He is our *stronghold!*

Chapter 6: God, Are You Up There?

The heavens declare the glory of God; the skies proclaim the work of his hands. Day after day they pour forth speech; night after night they reveal knowledge. They have no speech, they use no words; no sound is heard from them. Yet their voice goes out into all the earth, their words to the ends of the world. In the heavens God has pitched a tent for the sun. It is like a bridegroom coming out of his chamber, like a champion rejoicing to run his course. It rises at one end of the heavens and makes its circuit to the other; nothing is deprived of its warmth (Psalm 19:1-6).

I remember when I was a little girl lying in the cool grass on warm summer days, looking up into the sky and seeing the most interesting creatures in the cloud formations. I would see horses, whales, cities, funny man's faces with beards, and in my little girl mind, I would say to myself, "I wonder if God is up there?"

The message is the same every day: the sky, the clouds, stars and sun, from sunrise to sunset—they speak loudly of the majesty and glory of our Father! Even as a little girl, I had a deep longing for Him and I knew He was there! And He waited for me. *His faithfulness was in the waiting.*

On those hot, summer nights my mother would have me say a prayer that went something like this, "Thank You, God, for the birds that sing; thank You, God, for everything." Now as a grown woman—the woman of God He tells me I am—on those warm summer mornings I grab my cup of coffee, walk out on my porch, look up at the sky, smile to myself, and say, "Now I *know* the God who created those puffy clouds with all those whimsical characters—He's my Dad!" The skies pour forth speech at the work of His hands day after day without saying a word.

I recall that little prayer that my mother had me pray every night, and now I look up toward the heavens and I can say, "Thank You, Daddy, for the birds that sing, thank You, Daddy, for everything!" I'm so grateful that He delighted in me when I was that little girl, and that the God who created the whole universe still delights in me! I'm so thankful that He waited for me! *His faithfulness is in the waiting!*

Chapter 7: Speak to Yourself Loudly

Unrelenting Hope

I remember a time when I would lie in bed with all the shades drawn, shutting myself out from the world, welcoming the shadows of the night so the torment of the day would end. But the dark watches of the night only brought the voice of the enemy speaking lies that nothing good would come of my life; that nothing good would ever happen to me. I felt worthless, helpless, and unlovable, the lies were unrelenting. There was no hope for me.

I was worn out from my tears and my deep longing for my Papa. I cried out to Him for the kindness and comfort of His love. Somehow I would manage to open my Bible and turn to my beloved Psalms and read:

> Why, my soul, are you downcast? Why so disturbed within
> me? Put your **hope** in God, for I will yet praise him, my
> Savior and my God (Psalm 42:5).

It was as if I was a little girl looking down at my feet and He tipped my chin up—not to scold me, but to kiss and hug and comfort me, just like loving Daddies do. When I first read this in the Word, I realized I could speak to my soul the way that the psalmist did. Three times the psalmist recorded how he spoke to himself when he was discouraged and depressed. So I began doing the same thing; speaking to my soul and encouraging myself—speaking joy and peace, encouraging myself when there was no one else to encourage me. I would say, "Put your hope in God, Marj, for I will yet praise Him!"

***

Hope is a spiritual force, it is not wishful thinking. Hope is powerful because its strength is in Father God's faithfulness. Learn to expect something good to happen every day in your "ordinary, beautiful life!" Hope is a goal setter; it's the vision of what God wants for you:

> "For I know the plans I have for you," declares the Lord.
> "Plans to prosper you and not to harm you, plans to give
> you hope and a future" (Jeremiah 29:11).

God created every person with a need to have purpose in their life. Hope and faith work together for believing the plans and the future that God has for your life. Is it any wonder that the enemy tries to bombard our minds with feelings of despair, discouragement, and hopelessness? His ultimate plan is to steal our future, our destiny—what we were created in God to do. And if we have lost hope we lose the ability to believe for our future.

I didn't realize the importance and the power of hope until the waves and breakers of depression and despair began washing over me and I was tossed about in a dark, insecure, fearful ocean of hopelessness. I felt as if I was about to drown in this stormy, fierce season of life with no one to rescue me. And then I read about my anchor.

The Anchor Holds! Chained to Hope

> We have this certain hope like a strong, unbreakable anchor holding our souls to God himself. Our anchor of hope is fastened to the mercy seat which sits in the heavenly realm beyond the sacred threshold, and where Jesus, our forerunner, has gone in before us. He is now and forever our royal Priest like Melchizedek (Hebrews 6:19-20 TPT).

The purpose of an anchor is to keep a ship safe and secure at a desired location or to help control the ship during bad weather. No wonder I was feeling so insecure and out of control, I had disconnected myself from my anchor! If we disconnect from the anchor we will drift aimlessly, being tossed to and fro by every wind and wave of life.

Hope is the anchor that keeps us connected to God and His faithfulness! Anchors keep us steady and in one place where the winds and storms of life would otherwise shipwreck our lives. Our loving Father has given us great and precious promises to hold onto in His Word, and this is what holds us to Him. In the fierce storms of life, if we are not anchored securely to Him there will be nothing left of us, and we will literally "fall to pieces." If God doesn't hold us fast in His love, we will drown in the sea of our despair. Thankfully, in His faithfulness, God gave us an anchor—the name of that anchor is *hope,* and the chain is secured to the mercy seat!

Is it any wonder the enemy of our soul would want to steal our hope? Remember that God promises to give us a hope and a future? If the enemy can steal our hope (if that anchor isn't holding secure) then he can steal our future—our destiny and the dreams that Abba has planned out so carefully for each of our lives.

The enemy begins very subtly by bringing waves and currents of:

- Distractions
- Discouragements
- Worry/Anxiety
- Fear
- Depression

I have learned from the psalmist to speak to my soul and put my hope in God, making sure that my anchor is safe and secure once again.

Our Armor

I speak the promises of God to myself; after all, we listen to ourselves the most! For example, I might speak this verse over myself: "For no matter how many promises God has made, they are 'yes' in Christ. And so through him the 'Amen' is spoken by us to the glory of God" (2 Cor. 1:20 NIV). I also make sure that my armor is in place, and that the belt of truth is buckled securely around me so I am prepared to fight the good fight of faith with the Word of God, as Paul instructs us in Ephesians:

> Finally, be strong in the Lord and in His mighty power. Put on the full armor of God so that you take your stand against the devil's schemes. For our struggle is not against flesh and blood, but against the rulers, against the authorities, against the powers of this dark world and against the spiritual forces of evil in the heavenly realms. Therefore put on the full armor of God so that when the day of evil comes, you may be able to stand your ground and after you have done everything, to stand. Stand firm then, with the belt of truth buckled around your waist, with the breastplate of righteousness in place, and with your feet fitted with the readiness that comes from the gospel of peace. In addition to all this, take up the shield of faith, with which you can extinguish all the flaming arrows of the evil one. Take the helmet of salvation and the sword of the Spirit, which is the Word of God (Eph. 6:10-17).

We are to put on this six-piece set of armor—which is our Father's—and never take it off. I believe the Holy Spirit inspired Paul when He was writing this letter to the Ephesians to compare our spiritual armor with that of the Roman soldier's armor. However, the Roman soldiers had a seventh piece of armor. They had knee and leg protection called grieves. I believe that this is not included as a piece of our armor because the battle we fight is on our knees in prayer!

For our subject of hope, the piece of armor that I want to focus on is the belt of truth. The belt of truth holds all the other pieces of armor in place. It secures the breastplate of righteousness, which is the application of truth from the Word of God in our everyday lives. All of the other armor hangs on the truth of the gospel. It is the only piece of armor that completely surrounds us. We are to surround ourselves with the truth of God's Word. Jesus said He is the way, the truth, and the life. When we surround ourselves with Him, we are wrapped around with our loving Savior, protected and secure. Let's wrap that belt of truth securely around us.

> Let us hold unswervingly to the hope we profess, for He who promised is faithful (Heb. 10:23).

Hope is an expectation of something good, anchored in a faithful God. Hope finds confidence in the promise found in His Word. We have faith in that promise because faith can't work without love. And we surround ourselves with that promise by the belt of truth. Hope and faith come alive, and it becomes a powerful force as the love of God is poured into our hearts.

Remember that hope is always in the future. There are times when we've been full of hope, and there are times when we have been hopeless. We have to fight for hope! God promises in Jeremiah 29:11 to give us a hope and a future. So if our enemy can steal our hope, he has stolen our future, our destiny in God, and the purpose for which He created us.

I learned to speak to my soul when I felt hopeless, just like the psalmist did in chapter 42. Let's take a little closer look at this psalm.

It is interesting to note that this psalm was written by the sons of Korah. The sons of Korah joined David in many battles and had the reputation of being expert warriors, so we can imagine that David had a close intimate relationship with them. They became great leaders of worship alongside David, and they were leading the worship when David brought the Ark of the Covenant to Jerusalem. From warriors to worship, this is a striking example of how we should fight our battles today.

> As the deer pants for streams of water, so my soul pants for you, my God. My soul thirsts for God, for the living God. When can I go and meet with God? (Psalm 42:1-2).

Water is our life source and just as the deer is searching and panting for water this psalmist knows his soul can only be satisfied with the presence of God. We see his personal intimate relationship with His God as he calls Him "My God."

> My tears have been my food day and night, while people say to me all day long, "Where is your God?" These things I remember as I pour out my soul: How I used to go to the house of God under the protection of the Mighty One with shouts of joy and praise among the festive throng (Psalm 42:3-4).

Here he's probably recalling the time when he was leading the worship team in incredible, anointed worship as they were bringing the Ark of the Covenant into Jerusalem.

> Why, my soul, are you downcast? Why so disturbed within me? Put your hope in God, for I will yet praise him, my Savior and my God (Psalm 42:5).

In this verse it is evident that David is fighting a battle, but he's saying, "I'm not going to surrender to depression and discouragement! Soul, hear this: put your hope in God!" We also must fight the battle of hopelessness and speak to our soul. His Word—the truth—was teaching me to speak to my soul. I was learning how to fight the good fight of faith by preaching truth to myself. I knew that if the psalmist did it, so could I! I have the ability to encourage myself, preach to myself the Word of God (because Rom. 10:17 says that faith comes by hearing, and hearing by the Word of God), and believe in His promises!

We must surround ourselves with the truth of His promises and then we can be assured that the belt of truth is securely in place.

Here are five strategic ways I surround myself with the promises:

1. I write the promises of God in my journal.

2. I write them on index cards and put them in my pocket, my purse, on the fridge, in the car.

3. I text myself and set an alarm on my phone, reminding me to speak the promises of God to myself.

4. I take a picture of a highlighted verse in my Bible and I text it to myself.

5. I speak it into my audio recorder on my phone and I play it back to myself.

This is how I fight this battle when the storms of life threaten to overtake me. I say to myself, "Marj, put your hope in God!" We must fight this fight of faith when emotions of depression and discouragement seem to overtake us. We have to fight when our circumstances are oppressing and pressing down on us and we are full of turmoil! Understand that there are over 7,000 promises from God tucked in His Word. At the end of this section I have included some of the promises from the Psalms that I use for fighting this battle.

Protect Your Hopes and Dreams

God has great plans for our lives—bigger than we can even think or imagine! Sometimes those plans might come through a prophecy from another person or maybe God himself has put hopes and dreams in your heart. No matter where they come from, we must protect them.

> You will be secure, because there is hope; you will look about you and take your rest in safety. You will lie down, with no one to make you afraid, and many will court your favor (Job 11:18-19).

Here are some ways to protect your hope and dreams:

- Be careful who you share your dreams with. Hang out with other dreamers. Remember, our Dad says that we will become who we hang around with (Prov. 13:20).

- Don't allow criticism to come in (from yourself or others).

- Don't live in the past, it will only cause you to get in a rut. Hope is not in the past; it's always in the future.

- Thank God for the hope He pours into us by the power of Holy Spirit.

- Be careful not to look for praise. I have learned (sometimes the hard way) to be very careful not to seek approval from people—they make poor saviors!

- Every day when I wake up, I speak to my soul and say, "Something amazing is going to happen to me today!" This is what the promises of God have done for me. Instead of being a prisoner of depression and despair, I am chained to the mercy seat, protected and secure. **The anchor holds**!

A Necessary Ingredient: Patience

(Warning: It might be costly and extravagant)

> **Love** never gives up, never loses **faith**, is always **hopeful** and endures through every circumstance (1 Cor. 13:7 NLT).

In my walk with God, I have learned that I must develop patience (endurance and perseverance). Most people have the wrong idea about patience, and I've heard many people say, "Oh, don't pray for patience!" but nothing could be further from the truth! Patience is simply being consistently constant while we are waiting for something. Our faith teams up with patience—there is no faith without patience. When we say we believe one of the promises of God, what we need to do is to stand on that promise until it manifests in our life. *His faithfulness is in the waiting.*

This scripture says it best:

So do not throw away this confident trust in the Lord. Remember the great reward it brings you! Patient endurance is what you need now, so that you will continue to do God's will. Then you will receive all that he has promised (Heb. 10:35-36 NLT).

Learning patience (endurance) is a very extravagant and costly endeavor. It is a necessary ingredient to our maturity in Christ. And our Dad is very good at tailor-making our lessons on patient endurance to be specific just for us. I'm going to tell you about a true-life story that happened to me at the precise time when I was writing this section of the book.

My second son was addicted to drugs and alcohol. If you've ever have a child who has a problem with addiction, you will know exactly what I am talking about. This is how I learned patience and endurance. It was not optional; my son's life depended on it. Our God knows that mothers will fight to the end for their children; after all, He made us that way. My son struggled a very long time with addiction. He loved God and actually had more faith than any of my other children. When he was baptized in water at ten years old, a huge fish jumped out of the water behind him, and a prophetic word was spoken over him. From that day on we called him our, "Fisher of Men." This was an accurate description of him, with his charismatic personality. He loved people, and people loved him.

My son battled this addiction for many years. As a mother, the suffering of drugs or alcohol and pain can sometimes seem unbearable. When he was under the influence he would call, text, or post angry, accusing words that were shocking and hurtful at first. But as time went on, I realized this was not my loving, forgiving, witty, and amazingly creative son. Sometimes we did not hear from him for a few months, and when we did, he would say angry and hurtful things. But as I walked through this, I didn't care what he said—I was just thankful to hear from him because I knew he was alive. I poured over the scriptures and found comfort, hope, and the strength to forgive. As time went on, I learned how to battle for my son. This is how I developed patient endurance; I put my hope in God, I believed in His promises with the belt of truth tightly buckled around me, and took up the sword of the Spirit (see Eph. 6:17).

The Sword of the Spirit

The Roman soldier's sword was about twenty-four inches long and was very sharp on both sides. It was used for hand-to-hand combat. They trained rigorously until they became very skillful with this sword. Their lives depended on it—and so do ours. Our sword is the Word of God, and it becomes sharp as we put the Word in our minds, hearts, and mouths.

> For the word of God is living and active and full of power [making it operative, energizing, and effective]. It is sharper than any two-edged sword, penetrating as far as the division of the soul and spirit [the completeness of a person], and of both joints and marrow [the deepest parts of our nature] exposing and judging the very thoughts and intentions of the heart (Hebrews 4:12 AMP).

This is the way we can fight our battle in the heavenly places. We must always remember that our battle is not with people. We are to love people. Our battle is against principalities, powers, rulers of the darkness of this age, and spiritual hosts of wickedness in the heavenly places (see Eph. 6:12).

So my training was long and rigorous (Patience Training 101) I was learning to take my sword, find the promises in the Word of God, and aggressively smash strongholds in my son's life. This takes faith, putting our hope on the promises, and, yes, it takes patience.

Let me share with you the powerful results of this warrior mother's victory in my son's life as I let the high praises of God be in my mouth, and a two edged-sword in my hand (Psalm 149:6). My son sent the following text to me as I was writing this section on hope:

"Dear Mom, I wanted to wait until I had some accomplishments and sobriety under my belt before I reached out to the both of you. I've wanted to tell you both how much I miss and love you so much lately, but I've abused that privilege. So today please accept my sincere apology and know in your hearts and believe I am 100% sober and independent again. God is so unbelievably generous with His love, and is graciously patient with me. I signed a one-year lease recently, I live alone, and am working downtown again at a bistro. I hope all is well. I really miss you, and will work on making amends with others so I can fly there for the holidays this year. I am so sorry for the hurt I've caused. I never want to feel that pain again...Knowing that I hurt you both like that was the worst feeling I've ever felt before."

His faithfulness is in the waiting!

Here is a handy acronym for the word hope:

Hold Onto Promises Everyday

Promises from the Psalms

I always remind myself of this scripture when I am ready to put the sword in my mouth:

> "Have faith in God," Jesus answered. "Truly I tell you, if anyone says to this mountain, 'Go, throw yourself into the sea,' and does not doubt in their heart but believes that what they say will happen, it will be done for them. Therefore I tell you, whatever you ask for in prayer, believe that you have received it, and it will be yours" (Mark 11:22-24).

However, there is a condition to this promise in verse 25:

And when you stand praying, if you hold anything against anyone, forgive them, so that your Father in heaven may forgive you your sins.

What Jesus is saying is that we need to make sure we do not have any unforgiveness toward anyone. If we do, we won't have any power when we speak to our mountains. (In this case, it is in declaring the promises of God over your life, your loved ones and your situations) Before I put the sword of the Spirit in my mouth and declare the promises of God, I ask the Holy Spirit to search me of any unforgiveness in my heart so that I can repent and forgive. Always take care of offenses and unforgiveness, they are power robbers!

***

These are some of my favorite promises in the Psalms. Search more out for yourself, and put the sword of the Spirit in your mouth!

> Blessed is the one who does not walk in step with the wicked or stand in the way that sinners take or sit in the company of mockers, but whose delight is in the law of the Lord, and who meditates on his law day and night. That person is like a tree planted by streams of water, which yields its fruit in season and whose leaf does not wither—whatever they do prospers (Psalm 1:1-3).

> Surely, Lord, you bless the righteous; you surround them with your favor as with a shield (Psalm 5:12).

> The Lord is my rock, my fortress and my deliverer; my God is my rock, in whom I take refuge, my shield and the horn of my salvation, my stronghold (Psalm 18:2).

> I sought the Lord and he answered me; he delivered me from all my fears. Those who look to him are radiant: their faces are never covered with shame (Psalm 34:4-7).

Taste and see that the Lord is good; blessed is the one who take refuge in him (Psalm 34:8).

The righteous cry out, and the Lord hears them; he delivers them from all their troubles. The Lord is close to the brokenhearted and saves those who are crushed in spirit (Psalm 34:17-18).

Trust in the Lord and do good; dwell in the land and enjoy safe pasture. Take delight in the Lord, and he will give you the desires of your heart (Psalm 37:3-4).

The salvation of the righteous comes from the Lord; he is their stronghold in time of trouble. The Lord helps them and delivers them; he delivers them from the wicked and saves them, because they take refuge in him (Psalm 37:39-40).

Whoever dwells in the shelter of the Most High will rest in the shadow of the Almighty. I will say of the Lord, "He is my refuge and my fortress, my God, in whom I trust." Surely he will save you from the fowler's snare and from the deadly pestilence. He will cover you with his feathers, and under his wings you will find refuge; **his faithfulness** will be your shield and rampart. You will not fear the terror of night, nor the arrow that flies by day, nor the pestilence that stalks in the darkness, nor the plague that destroys at midday. A thousand may fall at your side, ten thousand at your right hand, but it will not come near you. You will only observe with your eyes and see the punishment of the wicked. If you say, "The Lord is my refuge," and you make the Most High your dwelling, no harm will overtake you, no disaster will come near your tent. For he will command his angels concerning you to guard you in all your ways; they will lift you up in their hands, so that you will not strike your foot against a stone. You will tread on the lion and the cobra; you will trample the great lion and the serpent. "Because he loves me," says the Lord, "I will rescue him; I will protect him, for he acknowledges my name. He will call on me, and I will answer him; I will be with him in trouble, I will deliver him and honor him. With long life I will satisfy him and show him my salvation" (Psalm 91).

Praise the Lord, my soul; all my inmost being, praise his holy name. Praise the Lord, my soul, and forget not all his benefits—who forgives all your sins and heals all your diseases, who redeems your life from the pit and crowns you with love and compassion, who satisfies your desires with good thing so that your youth is renewed like the eagle's (Psalm 103:1-5).

***

Our Daddy is so very kind to us, His children. He has given us every spiritual blessing, all we have to do is believe that *His faithfulness is in the waiting.*

Chapter 8: A Psalm of LIFE

The Most Beloved Psalm

The Lord is my shepherd; I shall not want.
He maketh me to lie down in green pastures:
he leadeth me beside the still waters.
He restoreth my soul:
he leadeth me in the paths of righteousness
for his name's sake.
Yea, though I walk through the valley of the shadow of
death, I will fear no evil:
for thou art with me;
thy rod and thy staff they comfort me.
Thou preparest a table before me
in the presence of mine enemies:
thou anointest my head with oil; my cup runneth over
Surely goodness and mercy
shall follow me all the days of my life:
and I will dwell in the house of the Lord forever.
(Psalm 23 KJV)

I used to think this psalm was about death; you know, the one that is read at just about every funeral or at the bedside of a dying person. But now I know this as a psalm about life—life, love, intimacy, security, contentment, and belonging!

A shepherd takes such good care of his sheep they never lack for anything. My Daddy left the ninety-nine to rescue me when I was in my rebellion.

> What do you think? If a man owns a hundred sheep, and one of them wanders away, will he not leave the ninety-nine on the hills and go to look for the one that wandered off? And if he finds it, I tell you the truth, he is happier about that one sheep than about the ninety-nine that did not wander off. In the same way your Father in heaven is not willing that any of these little ones should perish (Matt. 18:12-14).

He loved me so much that He would never let me go! His compassion and love overwhelmed me and overtook me as He pursued me for over twenty years—quietly, gently, lovingly, never condemning, never harsh, never giving up on me! He was always leading me into the way of His Son, into forgiveness and love.

Rescue! That's what good shepherds do. When a sheep falls into a ditch, the only way they can get back out is when the shepherd picks them up and puts them back upright on their legs. Oh, those darn ditches of insecurity, cares, anxiety, discouragement, failure, and despair! The Shepherd's eye is always on His sheep to rescue and lead them back into green pastures to feed on the Word, and to dwell beside the still waters of peace.

A herd of sheep will drink of the dew in the green pastures early in the morning. The Lord has trained me to come early in the morning to drink from Him and His Love Book. That's how it's been every morning for many years, just the Father and I. He quiets my soul, restores my hope, increases my faith, and leads me into truth—and contentment and peace floods my soul. I can say along with apostle Paul that I have learned to be content with much and with little because He strengthens me with His very own spirit. I shall not want as I drink deeply of God's love. I will love Him and worship Him forever because He first loved me. I can make it through anything with the One who makes me who

I am. I am being made more like my Daddy; I can see the resemblance more and more every day!

***

> "God gives us the vision, then he takes us down to the valley to batter us into the shape of the vision, and it is in the valley that so many of us faint and give way. Every vision will be made real if we will have patience."[1]
> — Oswald Chambers

It has been through trudging down the valleys of life (with my combat boots on) that He has taught me not to fear. I have experienced how faithful and loving my Father really is. Through a failing marriage, children who struggle with identity and rebellion and addiction, a baby who was near death at birth, financial burdens, and betrayal by friends and family members. I found the strength in the valley from the Good Shepherd, and somehow He used all things for my good. As I look back, these have been the most intimate times with my Daddy because He was close beside me. His faithfulness has always been in the waiting. Now I am able to comfort others with what I have been through as His life flows from me. God was never in a hurry when He was leading me through the valley to the high places, because I had so much to learn along the way. I remember how His love and His Word lit up my path, giving me strength and wisdom and the courage not to fear. Why? Because He was with me. When I was exhausted and overwhelmed, He would carry me off into a place of intimacy. He was never too busy—always available. In fact, He is deeply longing for my love. The deepest longing in my soul has been satisfied by my Father God! I belong to Him and He belongs to me. I am His beloved and He is mine.

I'm so grateful that my Daddy God showed me that the Christian life is not about rules and laws, but about the most intimate relationship available to all mankind. He sent His son to die for us, that's how much He loves us!

---

1. Oswald Chambers, *My Utmost for His Highest*, devotion for July 6th, (Dodd, Mead, & Co.: 1927).

Learning to Love Difficult People: His Provision?

Even in the valley of fear and uncertainty I have clung to God's promise that He is with me and that He will never leave me. In the valley of life is where I have grown the most. He has provided difficult people so I can learn how to love. This way, the enemy's spirit of cold love did not get a grip in my heart. The Lord taught me to humble myself and love my enemies. I remember very well when He first taught me this lesson. A family member owed me a sizable amount of money, and it became apparent they did not have any intention of paying me back. Unforgiveness and bitterness began to grow in my heart. But because God is the Good Shepherd, He led me right to His Word where it talks about about loving my enemies, praying for them, and blessing them by lending to them without expecting anything back (Luke 6:26-32). I remember the indignation that I felt in my heart and God reminded me how much I have been forgiven from and how He was teaching me to be like Him—merciful, kind, and forgiving. Was it God's provision to teach me how to love and pray for my husband while I was waiting for the Lord to deliver and heal him and set him free from anger? I've learned from experience that His faithfulness is in the waiting.

I learned how to fight my battles because of the lessons and training in the valley. I would open up the Word and hang out with David, Joshua, Sarah, and Esther—and I was amazed and astonished to find that they went through the same training! But God was right beside them (because He promised that He would be) to encourage them to be strong and courageous. I remember asking God, "Why, Daddy?" And He responded, "To develop unshakable faith in you, Pearl just like I taught them." That's where I learned to trust—in the valley. I learned that my heavenly Father is always with me and will never leave me, not like my dear father was taken in death from me. No, never leave me—the greatest promise of all!

A Cardinal, Pearl?

One memorable spring day the Lord taught me what I believe to be the greatest and most precious promise about how He will never leave me and that He is always with me. I was deep in the valley of depression, discouragement, and loneliness, and I doubted that He was with me. So I asked Him for a cardinal. He said, "A cardinal, Pearl?" I remember asking that if He was *really* for me and was *really* with me, to please send a colored bird to my bird feeder. I had never seen a cardinal at my bird feeder, so I was really testing Him by asking Him to send me a cardinal. How delighted the Lord must have been when the next day I stood with tears running down my face looking out my window at a beautiful red cardinal at my bird feeder!

> Yea, though I walk through the valley of the shadow of death, I will fear no evil; for thou art with me (Ps. 23:4 KJV).

Always with me—always faithful—He will never leave me. It's the greatest promise of all—that's my Dad! His faithfulness is in the waiting.

Many years later, I still smile whenever I see a cardinal, God's special gift to me. At our new home there is a pair of cardinals that visit us every day. I never tire of seeing them. But I don't need a cardinal anymore, because I believe God's promise to me that He will never leave me and that I am never alone. I am not fatherless because I am His daughter, His Pearl.

Stuck in a Rut

As a Good Shepherd, God leads me in paths of righteousness. This is fresh, new revelation! My spirit is excited when I find truth in His Word and it sets me free and strengthens me. He's taught me that a cellphone devotional isn't enough; it doesn't satisfy my soul. It is being alone with Him and His Word that tells me the truth of who He is and who I am. I am more in love with Him every day. I have to spend time with Him first thing in the morning, every morning. If I begin a load of laundry or start picking up the house or pack some quick lunches, the next thing I know, six children are clamoring down the stairs for my attention and I have lost that precious time with my Papa. When the house and laundry become my priority in the mornings, I get stuck in a rut.

Ruts are established by going back and forth, back and forth. Spiritual ruts happen when I am chasing my own way and I remain unsatisfied and unable to move on in my faith because I became stuck in a rut. Laundry, texts and emails to answer, lunches to make, and clutter in the house are all screaming for my attention. Day after day, they can pull me away from my Papa, and that rut becomes old, polluted ground—dry and arid and dusty with no growth, no life. These are the times when I've been like a stubborn, willful sheep thinking my way is the right way, only to realize I've dug a rut for myself.

Then my Shepherd comes to rescue me. Scolding me gently and tenderly for wandering away from Him. If I had continued going my own stubborn, "sheep-like" way instead of allowing Him to guide me with His rod and staff, I would have led myself into a broken marriage and kept wandering around like a lost sheep. I quickly learned the very first thing to do in the morning; like sheep, I delight in the dew of the morning. Drinking deeply for my day, for my life really, and I hang out with David in the Psalms every day.

Sometimes I just sit quietly with Him and listen to Him tell me how much I'm loved and accepted, how there's no need to compare myself with others. He has set me free by His perfect love—always leading me, guiding me in honor and respect, and setting me free from offense, unforgiveness, and bitterness. I am learning to love. I have found a place of rest and trust, contentment, and peace—that is what can be found on the path of righteousness. In quiet confidence, I have learned the greatest satisfaction and purpose of my life: pleasing my Dad and loving Him with everything that I am!

Those Darn Bugs

A sheepherder pours oil over the head of the sheep to rid them of bugs and flies that will lay eggs in their nostrils which eventually go to their brain and make them feel crazy (they will literally bang their heads against a fence post or tree). During my worship times, God pours that fresh oil of anointing over me lest those darn bugs make me crazy and devour me with doubt, fear, unbelief, and worry. His relentless love and faith in His Love Book has taught me not to be fearful and to give my Daddy all my worries and anxieties.

I remember when we had sold our house and we were waiting for a new one to be built. I was lying on a cot in a small camper and fear began to overtake my mind. Thoughts assaulted me like "What if we don't have enough money to finish the house? What if we have to live in this small camper through the winter apart from our three young sons? What if? What if?" God invaded my thoughts and interrupted the liar of fear, and suddenly, like a scared little girl, I meekly said, "Daddy can I get in bed with you?" And He answered, "Of course, precious Pearl." I knew I was surrounded by Him in His arms of safety, and that the big 'ole liar of fear couldn't scare me again. Ever since that night, when fear jolts me into wide-eyed sleeplessness, I still say, "Daddy, can I get in bed with You?" The answer is always yes! While the dark night is disappearing into the light of the dawn, I am safe in His arms. He longs for my love, and I yearn for His love. I am overwhelmed! I am His and He is mine.

Ouch! Those Briar Patches are Painful

Sometimes I wish I could just remember to walk closer to God! My own stupidity and stubbornness lead me into the briar patches of life (just like a sheep) and the entanglement seems so enormous and hopeless. But there He is, the Good Shepherd, waiting for me, His Pearl, to come and cry on His big shoulders and put my head on His chest until I feel His heart beating with love for me, just like the strong arms of an earthly Dad. That's how I always imagined it would be!

He is the Good Shepherd, and he has never forced himself into my life. I remember when I was afraid that I would have to give up partying, the pursuit of money and success, and thinking that a man would satisfy my life. But after my first husband died, this lost sheep came running into the Father's arms and His loving presence invaded my life. I can say along with Isaiah, that I was ruined for anything else. His faithfulness was in the waiting.

God never demanded that I gave up anything; I laid my life down willingly because now my yearning, wounded soul was satisfied and the Good Shepherd was now mine and I was His. The long, dark, wearisome search was over, and I knew that I was loved just for being me. He waited for me and was faithful. I had made such a mess of my life, but He dried my tears. I received God's wisdom and council, and by the end of our time together, I was filled with hope and joy as He told me how to untangle my mess, PEACE BY PEACE.

Two Friends Follow Me Wherever I go

When I am full of fear, I lay my head against His chest once again, and all my fears and worries are gone because His love never fails. He promised that goodness and mercy will follow me every day of my life. They are my constant companions. I live in the Lord's presence every day, hanging on His every Word. He is the one constant in my life; when a marriage seemed hopeless, children were rebelling, jobs were lost, and nothing seemed right in my life, I sat on my Daddy's lap and I knew that I shall not want for anything! I am loved, I belong, I'm accepted and I am approved of by the Good Shepherd.

His faithfulness is in the waiting!

Chapter 9: It's Time—It's Preparation Time

Forever I will lift up my soul into your presence, Lord.
Be there for me, God, for I keep trusting in you.
Don't allow my foes to gloat over me
or the shame of defeat to overtake me.
For how could anyone be disgraced
when he has entwined his heart with you?
But they will all be defeated and ashamed
when they harm the innocent.
Lord, direct me throughout my journey so I can
experience your plans for my life.
Reveal the life-paths that are pleasing to you.
Escort me along the way;
take me by the hand and teach me.
For you are the God of my increasing salvation;
I have wrapped my heart into yours!
Forgive my failures as a young man,
and overlook the sins of my immaturity.
Give me grace, Lord!
Always look at me through your eyes of love—
your forgiving eyes of mercy and compassion.
When you think of me,
see me as one you love and care for.
How good you are to me!

When people turn to you,
they discover how easy you are to please—
so faithful and true!
Joyfully you teach them the proper path,
even when they go astray.
Keep showing the humble your path,
and lead them into the best decision.
Bring revelation-light that trains them in the truth.
All the ways of the Lord are loving
and faithful for those who follow the ways
of his covenant.
For the honor of your name, Lord never count my sins,
and forgive them all—lift their burden off of my life.
(Psalm 25:1-11 TPT)

How can I accomplish my destiny and purpose for what my Daddy created me to do unless I cooperate with Him when He desires to take me to places beyond where I am. God knows exactly when to bring change into my life, and He knows what my character needs at the precise moment.

My Daddy whispered to me, "It's time. It's preparation time." So I knew that I must take time off from teaching. I didn't know the shaping and the newness of what was to come, but I knew if I was to go beyond where I was, I must obey Him. The same Spirit of the One who washed the disciple's feet lives inside of me. This was a time to for me to truly live by faith and believe that I am hidden in God, in the secret place—shaping, molding, and forming. I knew I was going to a place beyond.

> Now to Him who is able to [carry out His purpose and] do superabundantly more than all that we dare ask or think [infinitely **beyond** our greatest prayers, hopes, or dreams], according to His power that is at work within us (Eph. 3:20 AMP).

To go beyond—this was the purpose of this season. To go beyond requires change and stepping out of my comfort level. Repentance. Holiness. A setting apart. Being filled and flooded with the Holy Spirit. Experiencing more and more of His love, intimacy, and revelation from His Word. I knew He would be faithfully waiting for me and praying for me, just like He prayed for Peter in Luke 22:31-32, "Simon, Simon Satan has asked to sift you as wheat, but I have prayed for you, Simon that your faith may not fail, and when you have turned back, strengthen your brothers."

> "I am sure there are many Christians who will confess
> that their experience has been very much like my own
> in this, that we had long known the Lord without
> realizing that meekness and lowliness of heart are to be
> the distinguishing feature of the disciple as they were of
> the Master. And further, that this humility is not a thing
> that will come of itself, but it must be made the object of
> special desire and prayer and faith and practice."
> **—Andrew Murray**

Separation to Bring Preparation

I would cry out to the Lord, "Change me! Change me!" I felt confident and trusting and secure in our relationship to ask Him to change me. Only He can change me! The deepest desire of my life is to have more intimacy with my Abba. He brings circumstances into our lives to purify us. This is a time to lay our lives on the altar and surrender everything to Him. And as we surrender, it is like we are being purified on the threshing floor.

The purpose of the threshing floor in Bible times was to separate the wheat from the chaff. In other words, when the wheat goes through the threshing floor process it is then ready to be used. This is the same for us, when our sin is separated from us, we are ready to be used to help other people. As this happened in my life, a quiet confidence began to grow in me. I began to believe—truly believe—that God is the author and finisher of my faith.

I could trust Him. And there is nothing that satisfies more than to know you are doing what you were created to do.

After our threshing floor experience, we are purified to enter the Holy of Holies. We are moving out of the flesh into the spirit for true kingdom living. We begin to lift our hands in worship and the period of waiting is over. His faithfulness is in the waiting. The supernatural intimacy that we've only dreamed of with our God is about to take us *beyond*.

> For God speaks again and again, though people do not recognize it. He speaks in dreams, in visions of the night, when deep sleep falls on people as they lie in their beds. He whispers in their ears (Job 33:14-16a NLT).

I was looking back in my journal ten months earlier, before God gave me a dream that I am about to share, and I had written: "Pray for a heart of purity, holiness, and cleansing. Pray that I am becoming who He wants me to be and that I will yield. Pray for more visions, dreams, prophetic words, words of wisdom and knowledge. Open the eyes of my heart, Lord. And I pray that I would minister out of a place of love in the Father's heart, not out of pride, forgive me Father God when I have ministered out of self-righteousness. I pray that I minister from a position of humility, it is a great privilege that I even get to this! I submit myself to You for the transformation of my character by the renewing of my mind through your Word."

You too, can pray this same prayer. Here is a list of prayers I was praying right out of the Word:

> Turn my eyes away from worthless things; preserve my life according to your word (Psalm 119:37).

> Keep your servant also from willful sins; may they not rule over me. Then I will be blameless, innocent of great transgression. May these words of my mouth and this meditation of my heart be pleasing in your sight, Lord, my Rock and my Redeemer (Psalm 19:13-14).

I call to you, Lord, come quickly to me; hear me when I call to you. May my prayer be set before you like incense; may the lifting up of my hands be like the evening sacrifice. Set a guard over my mouth, Lord; keep watch over the door of my lips (Psalm 141:1-3).

(I) continually ask God to fill (me) with the knowledge of his will through all the wisdom and understanding that the Spirit gives, so that (I) may live a life worthy of the Lord and please him in every way: bearing fruit in every good work, growing in the knowledge of God, being strengthened with all power according to his glorious might so that (I) may have great endurance and patience, and giving joyful thanks to the Father, who has qualified (me) to share in the inheritance of his holy people in the kingdom of light. For he has rescued (me) from the dominion of darkness and brought (me) into the kingdom of the Son he loves, in whom (I) have redemption, the forgiveness of sins (Col. 1:9-14).

He Whispered in My Ears in the Night

While I was in the season of this threshing-floor experience, God gave me a dream—a vivid, memorable dream. Let me review a few points of wisdom about how to handle dreams.

- Before anything else, **pray**. Ask God if this dream is from Him; if so, ask Him to help you with the interpretation.

- I always **write it down** in my journal. I have a friend who has a journal that they only use to write down dreams. I have to write it down so I don't forget even the smallest of details. Remember, I just shared that I had prayed and asked Father God for more dreams.

- I share my dreams with a godly friend who has studied dream interpretation. It is wise to get **godly counsel**.

- If I have determined that this dream is indeed from God, it is extremely **vivid** in my mind and I will remember it years later. Sometimes it's a prophetic dream about something that is going to happen in the future, or it is to get my attention about a lesson He is trying to teach me.

- Finally, I look to see if the interpretation lines up with the **Word.** The Bible is our standard for *all* things.

In this dream, my friend Lori told me to sit down in a chair and then she placed a white towel at my feet in front of me. She told me to bend over the towel until my hair touched it. She said she was going to condition my hair with a special oil treatment and instructed me to let it saturate every hair and leave it on for a very long time. I remembered that I caught a glimpse of the red tube she had used on a side table beside the chair I was sitting on. I asked her, "How much do I owe you?" She replied, "Nothing; it's free."

My friend who is knowledgeable about dream interpretation helped me with the following symbols:

My friend Lori: In the dream, Lori was not representing my close friend, but it was the meaning of her name that was important: **The name *Lori* means "laurel tree" or "sweet bay tree, a symbol of honor and victory."**

White towel: The color white means purity.

Towel: The towel represents humility in this dream. In John 13:4, Jesus wrapped a towel around Himself and He washed the disciple's feet.

Hair: A covering of one's glory

Oil: Power and Anointing

Red tube: The color red symbolizes the blood of Jesus

"It's free": Lori had told me I didn't owe her anything. God's love is a free gift.

This dream was probably the most life-changing and profound dream God has ever given me. It was exactly what I needed during this time on the threshing floor. Now I have a visual in my mind when I need to remember that strength, power, and anointing is always available to me as I humble myself before Him.

Humility is the most beautiful characteristic of His Son. Humbling Himself to save all of mankind, becoming obedient even in death. Humility is designed to lift us up to find grace and favor. We must choose to wear it every day just like we would wear a warm coat to protect us against the elements of a cold, frigid winter's day.

> Therefore, as God's chosen people, holy and dearly loved, clothe yourselves with compassion, kindness, **humility**, gentleness and patience (Col. 3:12).

I must wear humility to protect me from all the worries and cares and anxieties of my life, giving God all my anxieties and worries and leaving them at His feet. I humble myself and say, "Daddy, I can't solve these problems, but I know You can. And so I roll them over onto your shoulders: big burdens and little burdens." I know if I do not roll my burdens onto my Father's back, they will surely break mine!

I was so excited when I found this scripture that described my dream:

> If you bow low in God's awesome presence, he will eventually exalt you as you leave the timing in His hands. Pour out all your worries and stress upon him *and leave them there*, for He always tenderly cares for you (I Peter 5:6-7 TPT).

Sometimes I am successful when I give my Daddy all my anxieties and worries, and sometimes I fail when I pick them back up again. But He is never-changing and He has never failed me, so I roll them back onto Him again. I trust my Daddy. Trust has been a difficult thing to overcome in my life because of people who have let me down. But I have learned through experience with my Father that I can always rely on Him, and He is true to His word—He will never fail me! I am consumed with going deeper into His love every day. His faithfulness is in the waiting.

Chapter 10: No Longer Afraid

If it wasn't for my Dad, I would be discouraged
But I believe— I am no longer afraid

Psalm 27
The Lord is my light and my salvation—
whom shall I fear?
The Lord is the stronghold of my life—
of whom shall I be afraid?
When the wicked advance against me to devour me,
it is my enemies and my foes who will stumble and fall
Though an army besiege me, my heart will not fear,
though war break out against me,
even then I will be confident.
One thing I ask from the Lord, this only do I seek:
that I may dwell in the house of the Lord
all the days of my life,
to gaze on the beauty of the Lord
and to seek him in his temple.
For in the day of trouble
he will keep me safe in his dwelling;
he will hide me in the shelter of his sacred tent
and set me high upon a rock.
Then my head will be exalted
above the enemies who surround me;

at his sacred tent I will sacrifice with shouts of joy;
I will sing and make music to the Lord.
Hear my voice when I call, Lord;
be merciful to me and answer me.
My heart says of you, "Seek his face!"
Your face, Lord, I will seek.
Do not hide your face from me,
do not turn your servant away in anger;
you have been my helper.
Do not reject me or forsake me, God my Savior.
Though my father and mother forsake me,
the Lord will receive me.
Teach me your way, Lord;
lead me in a straight path because of my oppressors.
Do not turn me over to the desire of my foes,
for false witnesses rise up against me,
spouting malicious accusations.
I remain confident of this:
I will see the goodness of the Lord
in the land of the living.
Wait for the Lord;
be strong and take heart and wait for the Lord.

"Love is an everyday occurrence; it's in the little things.
It's in the everyday monotonous things of life that we
experience God's love."
— Sgt. Matthew Hotelling

It's in the everyday, monotonous things of life when we experience God's love and faithfulness—that's how our circumstances change, and, most importantly, that's how we change as we experience the love and faithfulness of God in the everyday things of life.

I had to trust God to change my husband. Looking back, it was a day-to-day display of God's faithfulness. You see, it's in the waiting. As my husband was changing, he had to wait for me to be able to trust him again—day by day, every day. He studied and prayed over the scriptures. "Husbands love your wives as Christ loves the church." He prayed for ways that he could love me the way Jesus loves the church. He gave me his time; he sacrificed his time to spend it with me. He studied my love language and loved me in the way that I understood love. He served me and was kind and gentle to me, even when I was not. He was patient when I was irritable. He was faithful to call me when he was going to be late because he knew I would be fearful that he wouldn't come home. He was gentle when I needed comforting. It was in the monotonous, everyday things of our beautiful life that he loved me like Jesus loves His church.

What was God doing in me during the waiting? He was changing me! We've heard the saying that we can't change other people. Well, there was a newsflash for me during this time: **we can't even change ourselves!** What a relief that revelation was when I realized that God is the only One who can change me! I could relax and stop fretting that I wasn't this or that and give my mind a break—and I could just enjoy my life.

God's faithfulness brought about a restored marriage that brings glory to Him, because that's what our Dad does—He restores everything that has been lost and everything that has been broken. Here was a marriage that was almost lost with two broken people, but He was changing us—two people becoming one. His faithfulness was in the waiting.

One Sunday I was ministering at our church and I asked everyone to stand up if they have been waiting for something, for one month? Two months? One year? Five years? Ten years? Twenty years? There were people still standing after the twenty year mark.

I asked everyone to sit down and I taught them about how His faithfulness was in the waiting. "What do I mean by that?" I asked them. I asked what some of the things were that they had been waiting for, and some of the responses were: healing, increase in finances, restoration of a relationship, and salvation of loved ones.

I told them that we all know God could just snap His fingers and it would be done, so why the wait? After some discussion, these are some of the answers they gave for the purpose of the wait:

- To develop our faith
- Healing of deep hurts
- To change us (develop our character)
- Training in righteousness
- Teach us to learn how to love (Him and others)
- Develop our relationship (intimacy) with Him
- Develop a love for His Word
- Develop our total dependency on Him

Can we relate to these answers? I'm sure there are many more reasons, but while we are waiting, we can believe and no longer be afraid because we will know that His faithfulness is in the waiting.

Before I got into the teaching of Psalm 27, I shared how all of this came about. I had been on a trip to Virginia with my niece to visit my sister (her mother). The next morning I was up early with a cup of coffee and my Bible and began reading Psalm 27. As I sat meditating on this psalm, it occurred to me that this trip had been a long-awaited answer to prayer as my sister and I had been estranged for quite some time. It was painful for me at times because she is twelve years older than myself and had been like a second mother to me.

I was overwhelmed with adoration and love as I recalled all the ways God was faithful to me while I waited for Him to bring reconciliation. He is faithful to us while we wait to see the manifestation of everything we are believing for. This book came into being as Holy Spirit spoke to me on that warm summer's morning and said, "My faithfulness is in the waiting."

Let's take a look at Psalms chapter 27.

Fear is the Greatest Enemy of Intimacy

In verse 1, David makes a declaration that the Lord is his light and his salvation, He is the stronghold of his life so why should he be afraid. He is encouraging himself when the battle is raging. We must encourage ourselves (remember: *speak loudly* to yourself) when fear begins to slither its way into our lives, and the enemy tries to intimidate us. David tells himself not to fear; in verses 2-3 we see that he is even confident that those enemies who want to kill him will be the ones who turn back. He is so confident that his God is surrounding him that he knows he won't be afraid.

Sometimes principalities and powers of darkness declare war on us and it seems as if we are surrounded. We know that they come only to kill, steal, and destroy us, so we must wake up our faith, take courage that our God protects us, and not be afraid. When intimidation comes and accusations and discouragement seem like they will overtake us, we will not fear! We must hold up that shield faith and do battle with our mighty sword, the Word of God.

In verse 4, David says that He wants to live so close to God, so He will take pleasure in his every prayer. We can also pray, "Lord, I want to dwell—I want to live there in Your presence. I'm going to focus on You and not my circumstances. I'm not going to think about or talk about how hurt I am, how discouraged I am, how depressed I am that nothing is happening." And when the devil tells me that faith isn't working, I'm going to tell him to get out of my head: "Get out of my head, devil! I know who I am and I know who my Father is!"

I'm going to spend time with my Daddy. I'm going to wake up my faith—that sleeping giant of faith—and spend time in His Word. I'm determined and confident to walk by faith and not by sight. I'm believing what His Word says and I'm going to stir my faith up. I'm going to worship Him and thank Him and get my joy back—on purpose! I'm going to stay in His presence until I hear the Lord speak to me!

David was so confident because of his intimate relationship with his God, that he declared that his God *will* keep him safe and hide him when trouble comes. Where has He hidden me? In Christ! Yes, we can count on trouble coming—nobody is exempt from this. Jesus promised us that in this world there would be many troubles, but He went on to say, "Be of good cheer, I have overcome the world!" In other words, He is saying to us, "Have joy on purpose because I have made you overcomers as well" (See I John 5:4-5). Here John tells us that it is our faith that has overcome the world because we believe that Jesus is the Son of God. We are hidden in Him! Wake up your faith and believe the Word: Col. 3:3 tells us that we are hidden with Christ in God.

I had a vision one time of my Papa God lifting me high up on a rock to keep me safe. When I read Psalm 27, I can picture Him again (vs. 5) lifting me higher and higher on the big rock. Jesus was the Rock that He was lifting me on to—the same rock in the desert that Moses struck, and from it flowed living water in the middle of the desert. He is our rock of stability and security when it seems like everyone else has failed us. David compared Him to a fortress, a refuge, a shield, his rock. When the enemy surrounds us, He lifts us high up on a rock and will protect us from danger when we trust in Him. This is what He was doing while I was waiting: teaching me to trust that there is no other Rock like our God!

I remember during a woman's meeting I asked each woman there, "What does this mean to you personally when you think of the word *Rock*, for a name of God? What is the first thing that comes to your mind?" As each woman shared, I will never forget the most dramatic testimony that came from one beautiful, dark-haired young woman. She began to share that she used to be a drug addict before a friend invited her to church. She was actually high during the church service, and after she gave her heart to Jesus she was immediately delivered from the craving of alcohol and drugs. So her answer was the first thing that popped into her mind when she thought of the word *rock* was cocaine. She explained to us that the word *rock* was one of the street words for cocaine. But now, she told us that the drug she depended on had now been replaced with the Rock—Jesus. She was now "high" on that Rock, leaving all her shame and guilt behind. There was a very special bond between all of us that night and a new appreciation for knowing Jesus as our Rock!

David said that when He is high on this Rock, protected by his enemies, he will shout with joy! In fact, sometimes worship is a sacrifice, but David was going to worship, even when the enemy was breathing down his neck. This is the intimate place—the really close place—when we can hear the Lord's heart beating for us. What is this, the sacrifice of praise? This is what I have learned in the waiting, that I will praise and worship God, my Rock, even when I don't feel like it—when I just want to stay in bed, pull the covers up to my neck, and just watch TV all day. I have discovered that resting place of praise and worship; the place of mercy and grace when I am afraid.

This is my confidence, and I can strengthen myself the same way David did (vs. 13-14) and declare that I shall see the goodness of the Lord in all my circumstances. David has taught me that this is a way of life: To overcome fear, seek the Lord! This was his way of life. We read over and over again how David experienced intimacy with God and it delivered him from all of his fears. I draw out my sword when fear attacks with this verse: "He didn't give me a spirit of fear, but He gave me a spirit of power, love and a sound mind!" (See 2 Tim. 1:7)

David didn't give us a formula to follow. I think if he did, it is in our nature to follow that formula and forget about seeking an intimate relationship with God. That is why David exhorts us to seek God (vs. 14) because His faithfulness is in the waiting.

Ask God to teach you His ways when the enemy is breathing down your neck. So while you are waiting, pray. Carry this psalm around with you, and remember the promises given to us by King David while he was being chased by his enemies. Tell Papa God what you're afraid of and what you're facing. He didn't give us a formula, but He has promised in His Word that when we're afraid, He'll be with us! It is not only about getting answers—it is the seeking after God Himself, every day. Confident trust in our Papa is developed by our relationship with Him through our experiences of our everyday, beautiful life.

Make an Appointment

I am often asked, "What do you do when you spend time with God? I want to have that same close relationship, but I don't know how to start." First of all, it must be a priority and a commitment, make an appointment with God (just as if you would going on a date with your first love—because you are, you know). Secondly, there is no set time that I spend, it could be ten minutes or it could be two hours. It's all about developing an intimate relationship with your Abba Daddy. Here is a list of some of the things I might do on a typical morning with God:

- Become a lover of the Word of God! Be passionate about it. If you're not, pray and ask God to give you that hunger and passion for His Word. You know by now my passionate love for the Psalms, and I still read a psalm almost every day. I would recommend that you read through the Psalms (slowly, it's not a marathon) to learn about who God is and to understand the passion that David had for his God. Remember, you will become like the people you hang around with, so hang out with David in the Psalms and become a man or woman after God's heart!

- Holy Spirit might direct me to read something else in the Scriptures, but I do not use this time as a study time. This is my Daddy time. I love the prayers in Ephesians and Colossians and sometimes I make those a personal prayer for myself.

- I *always* spend time with God first before I intercede for other people.

- I tell Him of my fears, joys and concerns because He's my best friend! Some mornings I just thank Him for who He is and who He's making me to be.

- Sometimes I worship Him the entire time. I almost always have a time of worship and praying in the Spirit.

- I always listen. Sometimes I hear Him in my spirit, and other times I just know His presence.

- Beware of distractions! The enemy will bombard your mind with all kinds of distractions. That is one of the tactics he uses against us, but we must be aware of his schemes. Because I'm a doer and an organized person, my mind will get distracted by things that I need to do. Most of the time it's little things like you forgot to put tomatoes on your grocery list or I need to look at my calendar to check for appointments. I turn my phone off (put it in another room if it's too tempting to check it). One thing that I do that helps me is to keep a pad of paper next to me to jot down the things that pop into mind so I know I won't forget them when prayer time is over.

- Most of all, just enjoy Him and you will experience His faithfulness in the waiting!

Chapter 11: Delight Yourself

Make God the utmost delight and pleasure of your life
and he will provide for you what you desire the most
(Psalm 37:4 TPT).

The word *delight* refers to feelings of gratification, pleasure, or *joy*. Many of us have known this promise most of our Christian lives but probably we are more familiar with this translation: "Delight yourself in the LORD and he will give you the desires of your heart." We can all quote it, but have we put it into action? Have we experienced it in our lives? Do we really know what it means to delight ourselves in Him? I think we've all tried to "do" this because it is an incredible promise. I'm sure at different stages of our Christian walk this verse has taken on more meaning as the Holy Spirit brings us revelation.

Let's break this verse down a bit before I take us where I want to go with it. First of all, whenever we see *LORD* in all capital letters in the Old Testament, it is referring to a personal name of God. The Israelites would not even speak the name of Yahweh because they considered it too holy, so they are referring to Yahweh when they use all caps for *LORD*. To believers today, this is referring to God, the Father of the Messiah, our personal God to whom we can go boldly before the throne of grace. So we are to delight and take joy in our God, whom now we can call our Father too.

So now we have established that we are to take joy (delight in) our Father God in the first part of this verse. Now the second part is where we need more understanding: "And He will give you the desires of your heart." My understanding of the second half of this verse is much different now than when I was a new believer. There is a clearer, more distinct appreciation for what this means. As we delight and find joy in our relationship with Abba Father and develop an intimate relationship with Him, it shapes the yearnings of our heart and our desires start to line up with what Father God desires as our love and affection deepens in this passionate relationship. I could recognize when this was slowly and steadily taking place in my heart. As a babe in Christ, perhaps I inverted this verse to mean I would get the things I want if I just delighted myself in the Lord. But now thirty-five years later, I know the relationship with my Papa is shaping the desires of my heart. My heart desires what His heart wants for me. Perhaps the following will make this a bit clearer.

Joy on Purpose

The Spirit of the Sovereign Lord is on me because the Lord has anointed me to proclaim good news to the poor. He has sent me to bind up the brokenhearted, to proclaim freedom for the captives and release from darkness for the prisoners, to proclaim the year of the Lord's favor and the day of vengeance of our God, to comfort all who mourn, and provide for those who grieve in Zion—to bestow on them a crown of beauty instead of ashes, **the oil of joy instead of mourning**, and a garment of praise instead of a spirit of despair. They will be called oaks of righteousness, a planting of the Lord of the display of his splendor (Isaiah 61:1-3).

Some other words for *joy* are: delight, great pleasure, joyfulness, jubilation, triumph, exultation, rejoicing, happiness, gladness, glee.

He "bestowed on me the oil of joy"! (To bestow means to give a gift.) He anointed my head with joy when he took away my depression. I have had so much joy since that day that people tell me that I "glow." It's not because

I'm such a happy person; in fact, it really isn't part of my personality. I have quite a choleric disposition—I like to get things done and I like my requests to be done to my expectations. So I know this "joy" that I have is quite supernatural. The more joy I give away, the more He gives me. That's the spiritual principle of sowing and reaping.

The more I asked God about my destiny and purpose, the more He was silent—and the more anxious I became! And then one sleepless night He spoke to me down in my spirit (I call it my "knowing") and said, "My precious Pearl, don't be anxious and do not focus on that which is to come, I have a plan for you; will you trust me? This anxiety and worry is stealing your joy." Immediately my mind went to Philippians 4:4-7, which has been my favorite verse for a very long time, and wondered why I hadn't thought of this scripture before. That's what worry does—it will crowd out all the scripture that we *know* and have applied for years. In fact, worry is like a bully. Picture it elbowing out any scripture that you've ever known. Worry and anxiety will consume your mind, that's where the battle is, and it will steal your joy and your peace! But there's something more powerful in us: the Holy Spirit! That's one of His attributes, to lead us into truth—the truth that sets us free!

> Rejoice in the Lord always. I will say it again: Rejoice! Let your gentleness be evident to all. The Lord is near. Do not be anxious about anything, but in every situation, by prayer and petition, with thanksgiving, present your requests to God. And the peace of God, which transcends all understanding, will guard your hearts and your minds in Christ Jesus.

The Apostle Paul tells us two times to rejoice! The word *rejoice* can be defined as, "to feel or show great joy or delight." Do you see where Holy Spirit was taking me with this? He was saying, "Rejoice! Delight yourself in Me, and I will give you the desires of your heart. My plans and desires and *your* destiny will become the desires of your heart as you find great joy in Me!"

Rejoicing and feeling joy naturally finds its way into being thankful. You can't be joyful without being thankful! I dare you to try it.

That night when I went to bed, I started remembering (on purpose) everything that gave me joy that day. Isn't that what renewing the mind is all about? Then the next morning as I was spending my time with Papa, I looked at the astounding view out of our double windows and it looked like a mural painted on my wall. Oh, how I wish I could be as eloquent with my words as our God was with His paintbrush outside my windows! The pine trees were heavy with snow, bowing low to the ground as the wind whipped the snow around, bringing it back up again to the tops of the trees. It was as picturesque as a beautifully-choreographed ballet. For a brief moment, I caught a glimpse of a sparrow flitting and venturing out from its hiding place in the thickly-covered pine branches. So if my Papa's eye is on the sparrow, it is certainly on me.

I sat in my chair where I meet with my Abba every morning by the warm fireplace enjoying this "mural" in my home. It changes day to day—just for me, and I get to experience the hidden treasure of "joy on purpose."

My Abba protects me from taking these things for granted. He has protected me from selfish thinking by opening the eyes of my heart to "joy seeing." I can't explain it, but it sets me free from stress, anxiety, despair, and discouragement. I can see now with the eyes of my spirit that joy is in the relationship. Begin paying attention to the beauty around you.

Enjoyment in our Dad begins with the little things, it's part of developing that intimate relationship with Him. Ask Him to open your eyes—your spiritual eyes—so you can enjoy Him. You'll be surprised at what you "see." This happened to me a few years ago when I was mowing our expansive lawn of five acres. I remember sitting on our lawn mower and gripping the steering wheel tightly as I thought about all the other things I had to do that day and wishing this task would be over quickly. Then I looked up at the magnificent view of the valley below, the rolling green hills and the quaint little town below our property—it looked like a picture on a postcard. I stopped the mower and began drinking in this picturesque view that my Papa had given me, just for me. Did I begin thanking Him for this astounding view that I had taken for granted? Yes, but more importantly, I began thanking Him for opening my eyes so I could en**joy** what had been there all along. Suddenly, my anxious heart was filled with the wonderment of my intimate love from my Papa.

When the Apostle Paul wrote to the church at Philippi, he wanted them to understand that joy is in the journey. He was in prison with Silas when they were worshiping God and rejoicing ("joying") in Him and the prison doors flung open and their chains fell off! That's the power of joy! The chains of anxiety, stress, and worry fall off of us when we are "joying"!

"Rejoice in the Lord always, I will say it again: Rejoice! Let your gentleness be evident to all." When you have this kind of joy, gentleness is also a byproduct; after all, how can you be irritable and harsh when joy is overflowing out of you?

Are we so consumed with pursuing our destiny that we fail to rejoice along the way? If we do, we will quickly lose sight of our purpose. Joy (and gentleness) are fruits of the Spirit. This is the fruit—the joy fruit—of abiding in that intimate, all-satisfying relationship. If we lose sight of this, our vision is darkened and our quest for destiny only becomes worldly success. Joying on purpose will set us free to enjoy an intimate relationship with Father God.

That day I sat in my fireside chair with a snowstorm raging around my house and having a "suddenly" moment with my Papa. I experienced such joy in the landscape outside my window that I was so full of thankfulness! Tears welled up in my eyes as I asked His forgiveness for neglecting what the Lord had so carefully planned for me along this journey. Those words of forgiveness in my mouth and the tears streaming down my face all spoke of thankfulness as I "joyed" in Him. It was then I decided to start a "Joy Journal," exclusively set aside for recording my joy moments. Writing these down is important to me because it helps me not to forget the little things that give me strength. There's an old saying that says, "Be faithful in small things because it is in them that your strength lies."

Paul wrote about another fruit of the Spirit in this passage: Peace. He talked about the peace which transcends all understanding, a supernatural peace. The natural man has no understanding of this kind of peace. This kind of peace will even guard your hearts and your mind. And it is all because of joying! What a powerful weapon to use when the enemy attacks our minds: Joy on purpose. We must fight for joy! Joy is a spiritual weapon. Joy conquers depression, discouragement, selfishness, and anxiety. That's why Paul said we must always rejoice!

Worry makes you weary, but joy gives us strength. Who would have thought that joy could be a weapon? Remember, our mind is the battlefield. We must fight the good fight of faith. The enemy will come in and steal territory and occupy if we don't get control of our thoughts! This is like training for war in the physical. My son has learned in the Marines that the more he practices, the more precise his aim gets. The more dramatically his aim improves, the more confident he gets that he will be protected. In the spiritual realm, we are shooting down those thoughts before they can become a strong hold—a fortress. The enemy always knows the weak areas of his targets. What are your weak areas? Offense, unforgiveness, insecurity, an approval seeker, comparing yourself to other people, or rejection? Know your weak areas and fortify them with the Word.

Stand Guard

Let's use offense for an example of how the enemy comes in and tries to occupy our territory (our mind). Paul tells us in 2 Corinthians to always keep ourselves free from offense so Satan might not outwit us. Paul says we know his schemes, so we shouldn't be ignorant of his devices. Don't you just hate it when somebody tricks you? That's just what the devil does when we won't forgive an offense. Paul tells us that if we don't forgive, we've left an open door for Satan to come in. It gives him the legal right to come in and occupy our mind. When we won't let go of an offense, it seems like that is all we can think about. Am I right? I ask myself, "Why am I thinking about this?" Then when I get busy with something else, that thought just comes marching itself right back on through my mind—and taking my joy with it. It just replays over and over as we keep rehearsing it in our thoughts, and before you know it, it takes up a stronghold in us. That's how the devil works—leave the door open a crack, and he swings it wide open and brings unforgiveness and bitterness on along with it.

No matter how large or small the offense, it will cause the same damage and Satan will outsmart us. For example, take a small offense and let's see where it leads. Let's say I am in the grocery store shopping for my family, when a woman pushes her way past me to get the last head of lettuce that is on sale. I think, "Well that was pretty rude," but I smile at her and move on. Later the same woman heads to the checkout lane the same time as me, and just moves right on ahead of me, bumping my cart in her effort to beat me to the lane that just opened. Now I think, "Okay, that's just too much." Now I have to stand in line even longer because it looks like she has bought enough groceries for a month for two households! And to top it all off, now I will be late picking my daughter up from her dance class. So while I wait I start texting my friend and complaining about this terribly rude lady in the grocery store. Then I cross my arms and let out deep sighs—*loudly*—so everyone around me might share in my injustice. And when I finally pick my daughter up (late, of course) I apologize to her and tell her it really isn't my fault because there was a very inconsiderate woman at the store who pushed ahead of me and made me late. This has now thrown off my whole schedule, and I find myself clenching the steering wheel (Take note that when you are gripping your steering wheel tightly, you're probably anxious and stressed.) and fuming as I picture this lady's face in my mind. I rush home and put all the food away and start cooking dinner, and now my husband comes home from work to find me frantically trying to get dinner on the table before he has to rush off to take our son to soccer practice. I profusely begin to tell him how sorry I am, and now start telling him about the woman in the grocery store.

Sound familiar? We all have experienced these situations, whether at the grocery store, in traffic, or in the office. I know what the Apostle Paul would say to us, "Beloved this should not be!" This is how our enemy can take a small offense and outwit us! Notice in the above scenario that I could not keep this injustice to myself—I had to make sure that when I was waiting in line that everyone around me knew how irritated I was, so they could clearly see that this woman was in the wrong. Then I complained to my friend (yes, texting and posting on social media counts), my daughter, and my husband. Now I've also allowed the devil to add complaining to my offense. The enemy just set up a stronghold in my mind and stole my joy over a silly, insignificant offense that should have been forgiven immediately. I opened the door a crack, and he came right in and paraded my joy right back out. This is why it is so critical to take every thought captive and overlook an offense so that we will not be outsmarted by the enemy.

I don't know about you, but this makes me mad when I think that the enemy can build a fortress in my mind. I'm going to learn to use all my weapons. This is a discipline that we must develop so we don't allow our thoughts to take us just anywhere, especially in the area of offense. This is something that must be developed as we mature.

Let's look at this scripture passage again:

> Beloved friends, what should be our proper response to God's marvelous mercies? I encourage you to surrender yourselves to God to be his sacred, living sacrifices. And live in holiness, experiencing all that delights his heart. For this becomes your genuine expression of worship. Stop imitating the ideals and opinions of the culture around you, but be inwardly transformed by the Holy Spirit through a total reformation of how you think. This will empower you to discern God's will as you live a beautiful life, satisfying and perfect in his eyes (Romans 12:1-3 TPT).

This is the joy that David writes about, isn't it? Let's purpose to pay attention to our thoughts and live in holiness, not as culture around us does. We can't take up silly offenses that steal our joy and stunt our growth and, more importantly, our relationship with Father God. These have been the most important scriptures to me as I pursue my love relationship with my Papa. Becoming transformed means being changed from the inside out. If you change your thoughts you can change your life. It's all about loving God and loving people—and living a beautiful life, fully satisfied and content. This is joy on purpose!

If we need a checklist of what we should be thinking about, Paul gave us one in Philippians 4:8, which is so beautifully worded in *The Passion Translation*:

> So keep your thoughts continually fixed on all that is authentic and real, honorable and admirable, beautiful and respectful, pure and holy, merciful and kind. And fasten your thoughts on every glorious work of God, praising him always.

This list is easy to remember, and I often put my thoughts up against this list. We must train ourselves (remember that we're in a battle), by taking every thought captive. Every day I give Holy Spirit permission to give me a nudge and guide me in my thoughts. This is how we are changed, one thought at a time. Isn't that how we renew our mind? It's not that difficult. (Again, put this list that Paul has given us in your phone, on an index card—still my personal favorite.) We must be intentional if we are going to win the battle. However, we must also guard the gates of our eyes and ears and what we are putting into our mind as well, especially with the current onslaught of social media.

I have so much "joy fruit" because Holy Spirit anointed me with the oil of joy. When people ask me to pray for them, oftentimes Holy Spirit will direct me to impart joy to them. I pray for them and tell them I am giving them some of my fruit of joy, and I see the transformation before my eyes. Their countenance changes from a face characterized by worry and stress to one of joy. Sometimes they bubble over with so much joy that they can't stop laughing. That's the work of the Holy Spirit. That oil never stops flowing as long as I keep joying. I know that at this moment, every day, I am living my destiny! How do I know? I'm delighting myself in the Lord on the journey, and He is giving me the desires of my heart. I'm finding my purpose in joy!

Joy is the strength of my life. It is found in the innocent laughter of children and when family gathers together for the holidays. But it is also to be found in the mundane routine rituals of life—after all, these are more commonplace than children on Christmas morning, celebrating of your child's wedding, or the birth of a child. Finding joy on purpose in our everyday, ordinary, beautiful life is like searching for that rare, precious pearl. The Bible tells us that "where your treasure is, there will be your heart also." It's like the big adventure! Instead of succumbing to frustration, despair, and boredom in the Monday morning cleanup, our hearts will be strengthened as we look for joy on purpose! I find joy in the quietness of my house when my mind can rest from being pulled in ten different directions. I can glimpse out my front windows while I am picking up the half-eaten bowls of cereal from the table; I pause to capture the beauty of fresh snow on the pine trees—I linger there until the beauty catches my breath and I say:

> "Thank You, Papa God. Thank You for this fresh, white snow that makes everything brand new. The branches on the trees are moving ever so slightly—is that their praise to You? Thank You for the beauty of this landscape, but more importantly, thank You for opening my eyes so I might enjoy this moment in my day. Was this just for me, Papa? To remind me just as I am warm and protected in my home, I am always protected in your love?"

One moment in time brought me joy on purpose, and throughout the rest of my day I can worship and rejoice in the One Man who knows everything I ever did—and still loves me.

Now when all my children are grown and the house is quiet, I still experience this same joy as I listen to the crows squawking in my yard, and as winter has found its way back around (as it does every year), and the same pine trees are covered with snow, and another season in my life has made its way. But instead of yearning for the "the good ole days," I look forward to today so I can linger a little longer in my Papa's joy and thank Him for the constant, unfailing, consistent love that He has always shown me—never changing, always the same, always faithful. I look forward to tomorrow and the change of the seasons in my life, because then I will know Him even more than I do today.

Now my thoughts have been redirected to meditate on the beauty of the Lord. David said, "O that I may gaze upon the beauty of the Lord, all the days of my life." Is this the renewing of my mind? I think this is a setup for joy and contentment!

In Psalm 31, David pleads with God to restore the joy of his salvation back to him. *The Passion Translation* puts it so beautifully, saying that even during a crisis that he will be radiant with joy. This is joy on purpose. Even when we have sinned or someone else has hurt us, we can also be filled with praise for His love and mercy. David goes on to say that God has kept him from being conquered by his enemy. This is what I want you to understand, Beloved: Even the smallest of offenses (if we choose to take them) will damage our relationship with our Loving Papa, and our enemy will have just won the battle.

This is our ultimate joy—the joy of knowing we will spend eternity with our Papa, the joy that we have been made righteous, and that all our shame and guilt have been taken away and all our sins forgiven.

Joy on purpose, look for it in the everyday, ordinary, beautiful days of your life. If you don't you will become weak, discontent, and will look for love in all the wrong places. And what is our Papa doing while we are seeking joy on purpose? He faithfully waits for us. *His faithfulness is in the waiting!*

How to begin your joy journey:

1. Shop for a "Joy Journal." This is one of my favorite things to do! I always take my time and look through all the journals, and when I see it, I know it's the one! It's kind of like shopping for a new pair of shoes or a new handbag. It fits "just right" for my purpose.

2. Always date your entries. This is important when you go back and read them.

3. Keep it handy. Maybe next to your Bible or on your desk or bedside table. If you want to keep it private, then keep it in its own special place.

4. Don't think you have to write a whole page every day. Sometimes my entries are just one sentence. I might go a day or two without writing anything, and other days I might make three or four entries.

5. When something comes to your mind, put it on your notepad in your phone and make your entry later. If you're like me, you'll forget about it later. Nothing is too short, too silly, or too insignificant.

Let me give you my example of my post on Valentine's Day:

February 14th

Thank you, Papa God, that you are always the same in my life, you never change, whether I am up or whether I'm down. Your love for me never changes. This is my joy for today.

6. When you do mess up, ask for forgiveness, repent of taking up offense, and close the door to the enemy.

7. Begin your training in spiritual warfare: Guard your thoughts.

8. Memorize these or write them down:

I will think about:

- All that is authentic, real
- Honorable
- Admirable
- Beautiful
- Respectful
- Pure
- Holy
- Merciful
- Kind

Say this prayer with me, and copy it into your "Joy Journal":

El Sinkhat Gili—God, My Exceeding Joy
My Dearest Papa, my El Sinkhat Gili,
The deep longings in my heart cry out to know you more,
to know you on my good days, but especially on my really
bad days, that you are so merciful and kind to me and you
lift me up and comfort me in your strong arms and wipe
away my tears. You have helped me grow up so much,
Papa, that I run to you, my God of "exceeding joy" before
my anxious thoughts find their way into an abyss of
depression. I run to you first and you remind me of your
great kindness and mercy that I don't deserve but that you
have promised are mine. And as I just sit quietly with you,
pouring out my all my anxieties and troubles you fill me
with your joy! Not just "joy" but exceeding joy, because
that is who you are.
You are my El Sinkhat Gili!

Chapter 12: "The Pearl of the Psalms"

God of Heaven's Armies, you find so much beauty in your
people! They're like lovely sanctuaries of your presence.
Deep within me are these lovesick longings, desires and
daydreams of living in union with you. When I'm near you
my heart and my soul will sing and worship with my joyful
songs of you, my true source and spring of life! O Lord of
Heaven's Armies, my King and my God, even the sparrows
and swallows are welcome to build a nest among your altars
for the birds to raise their young. What pleasure fills those
who live every day in your temple, enjoying you as they
worship in your presence! (Psalm 84:1-4 TPT).

I can't write about having an intimate relationship with Father God
without discussing the intimacy of praise and worship. Spurgeon has
called Psalm 84 the "Pearl of the Psalms."

The greatest longing and desire of this psalmist's heart was to meet with
his God. That is our pilgrimage as well. We don't need more programs,
entertainment, or social clubs. The leaders in the church you attend must
be worshipers; we must expect to meet with our loving God—every time
we gather! This was the psalmist's longing, and it must be ours too.

When we worship, we are offering a sacrifice to God. Hebrews tells us to
continually offer up a sacrifice of praise to God. The animal sacrifices of
the Old Testament that once brought a pleasing fragrance to God have
now been replaced by our praise and worship. It goes on to say that we no

longer offer up animal sacrifices, but our praise and worship are the lambs we offer up to Him.

Set Free from Fear and Worry during Worship

Praise and worship is not only an intimate time with God, it is a powerful time that can break chains of bondage off of us. Paul and Silas are a quintessential example of this in the book of Acts, as they were set free from prison while worshiping God.

In Acts chapter 16 we see that a slave girl followed Paul and Silas for several days, shouting that they were servants of God and that they were telling people how to get saved. After several days of this slave girl following them, Paul was very annoyed and commanded the spirit of python to come out of her. The owners brought charges against Paul and Silas because the slave girl earned a lot of money for them. Paul and Silas were beaten, their feet and hands bound with chains, and they were thrown into a prison cell. They prayed and worshiped through the night and suddenly there was a great earthquake, and all the prison doors flung open. Their chains came off and all the prisoners around them were freed as well!

When I was worshiping at our church recently, the presence of God was very strong and I was overcome by God's love. For the next few days I felt different—lighter, happier, free. I noticed after that experience that I went through my days with no worry, concern, or anxiety. I knew I had been set free from fear and worry during that worship time! It's true! I had no more fear or worry. I was believing and declaring over myself the promise in Psalm 34:4: "He delivers me from all my fears." I love the Psalms!

Two days later my husband had a heart attack and was rushed to the hospital. All through the experience—the ride in the ambulance, to the doctors and nurses rushing around in the emergency room, and then into surgery—I had no fear or worry. It had been replaced with the peace that passes understanding. What a divine deliverance!

Did fear and worry try to attack me? It sure did! My husband had a heart attack on the same day that my mother had died, and the enemy did not neglect to remind of that. Also, he kept reminding me that my first husband had died of a massive coronary. I kept refusing those thoughts because I was not going to take the bait! After all the miraculous things God did for us during those few days, I can't imagine what I would ever have to be fearful of again! God's love kept flowing from all our family and friends who were surrounding us.

His perfect love was flowing through my sacrifice of praise and broke my chains, delivering me from fear and setting me free! Our worship is a sweet-smelling incense to God. And just like Paul and Silas, when we worship Him, our chains can be broken—and we break out of our prison too!

Conclusion

Beloved, pray, believe His Word, and don't ever lose hope for what you are believing for. He loves you; you are His child, and He is your Beloved Father. Believe His promises and allow your faith to grow. He desires an intimate relationship with you. Remember that He will do so much more than you can even imagine. Consider His presence to be your greatest need. He's always waiting for you. And remember:

His faithfulness is in the Waiting!

> And now we are brothers and sisters in God's family because of the blood of Jesus, and he welcomes us to come right into the most holy sanctuary in the heavenly realm—boldly and with no hesitation. For he has dedicated a new, life-giving way for us to approach God. For just as the veil was torn in two, Jesus' body was torn open to give us free and fresh access to him! And we now have a magnificent King-Priest to welcome us into God's house, we come closer to God and approach him with an open heart, fully convinced by faith that nothing will keep us at a distance from him. For our hearts have been sprinkled with blood to remove impurity and we have been freed from an accusing conscience and now we are clean, unstained, and presentable to God inside and out. So now we must cling tightly to the hope that lives within us, knowing that God always keeps his promises! (Hebrews 10:19-23 TPT).

About the Author

Marj Hotelling has been involved in ministry for many years and led many woman's Bible studies, and as a result, she has many spiritual daughters. She and her husband, Jamie, currently attend Third Day Worship Center in Syracuse, New York, where they serve in leadership. The Hotellings live in Central New York and have six children and six grandchildren.

Marj can be contacted at hotellingmarj@gmail.com.